THE

BREAKING

OF

CURSES

**Spiritual
Warfare
Series
VOLUME V**

Frank & Ida Mae Hammond

The Breaking of Curses, by Frank Hammond
ISBN # 0-89228-109-X

Copyright ©, 1993

Impact Christian Books, Inc.
332 Leffingwell Ave.,
Kirkwood, MO 63122
314-822-3309
www.impactchristianbooks.com

Printed in the United States of America

CONTENTS

INTRODUCTION

The subject of curses is worthy of our careful attention. The word "curse," in its various forms, is found over 230 times in the Bible. Six different words in Hebrew and three in Greek are translated "curse". These different words convey various aspects of curses. Any Bible subject with such extensive emphasis merits our close study.

From a realistic viewpoint it is obvious that many people lack evidence of God's blessings in their lives. The absence of God's blessing is evidence of a curse. We are either blessed or cursed; there is no in-between. We must determine "if" and "why" we are cursed and ascertain what must be done to reverse our condition. God has in Christ Jesus made provision for us to move from curse to blessing.

In the Old Testament, the most common word for "curse" is *arar,* which means to utter a wish of evil against; to call for mischief or injury to fall upon, or to bind with a spell.

From God's perspective, a curse is a sentence of Divine judgment upon sinners. It is the opposite of covenantal blessing. Curses result from breaking God's commandments. Thus, all the curse-sayings found in Deuteronomy, chapters twenty-seven and twenty-eight, are repercussions of one's violating his relationship to God. Announcements of Divine punishment identify curses imposed by God.

Another Hebrew word translated "curse" is *cherem* which designates things devoted to God or earmarked for destruction. Such things become a curse to those who take them for themselves. For example, Achan took spoil from Jericho, which was devoted to God, and it became a curse to him (See: Joshua 7). The tithe is holy unto the Lord (See:

3

Leviticus 27:30) and becomes a curse to the one who keeps it for himself (See: Malachi 3:8-10). An idol is a "cursed thing", and one who brings an idol into his house becomes cursed in a similar manner (See: Deuteronomy 7:25,26).

It is much too superficial to group the several Hebrew and Greek words under the one English word "curse". However, in this book we have avoided the technical distinctions of the Hebrew and Greek words and let the identification of different kinds of curses reflect the various aspects of curses.

The Breaking of Curses is published with a prayer that the truth disclosed will bring many from curses to blessings.

1

CURSES ARE REAL

The Bible affirms the reality of curses. God said that He will visit "the iniquity of the fathers upon the children, and upon the children's children, unto the third and the fourth generation" Exod. 34:7.[1]

As the Israelites saw these curses being passed down in their families, they devised this proverb: "The fathers have eaten sour grapes, and the children's teeth are set on edge" Ezek. 18:2. In other words, the children were suffering from the sins of their fathers. The generational curses which God imposed were real.

The Book of Judges records a curse that well illustrates the reality of curses. When Gideon died, he left seventy sons. Abimelech, one of his sons, murdered his brethren in order to secure the national leadership for himself. Only Jotham, Gideon's youngest son, escaped. Milo and Shechem sided with Abimelech. Therefore, Jotham pronounced a curse upon those who had slain his brethren:

> Let fire come out from Abimelech and devour
> the men of Schechem, and the house of Milo;
> and let fire come out from the men of Shechem,

---

[1] All scripture references are from the King James Version of the Bible unless otherwise indicated.

and from the house of Milo, and devour Abimelech...

Then **God sent an evil spirit** between Abimelech and the men of Shechem; and the men of Shechem dealt treacherously with Abimelech: That the cruelty done to the threescore and ten sons of Jerubbaal [Gideon] might come, and their blood be laid upon Abimelech their brother, which slew them; and upon the men of Shechem, which aided him in the killing of his brethren...

Thus God rendered the wickedness of Abimelech, which he did unto his father, in slaying his seventy brethren: And all the evil of the men of Shechem did God render upon their heads: **and upon them came the curse of Jotham the son of Jerubbaal.**

Judges, 9:20,23,24,56,57 (Emphases ours)

From the preceding account we learn several key truths:

(1) Curses are real. The curse pronounced by Jotham came upon Abimelech and his cohorts.

(2) The curse was caused by sin. Abimelech heartlessly murdered his seventy brethren.

(3) The curse was spoken by Jotham with an appeal for God to judge whether it was just. God is the judge of men's hearts and motives.

6

(4) God sanctioned the curse. Jotham's words alone were insufficient to curse Abimelech.

(5) The power of a curse is demonic. "God sent an evil spirit" to effect the curse.

From secular history we see that curses are real:

There were thousands of Jews living in Spain in 1480 at the beginning of the Inquisition, and within three years the expulsion of professing Jews was initiated. In 1492, the year Columbus sailed to America, King Ferdinand and Queen Isabella signed an edict expelling all Jews from Spain.

Spain became a great nation, extending her empire far and wide; however, Spain began to decline, and her empire disintegrated.

> She has never returned politically, economically or culturally to her former glory and is today considered one of the poorest nations of Western Europe.
>
> Furthermore, the people of Spain have never ever experienced a spiritual revival of any quantity or quality...As those believers laboring in Spain will tell you, it is one of the most spiritually dry nations in the world.
>
> Why all these adversities on this once great land? Could it be that God's law, "'I will bless those who bless you, and those that curse you will be cursed" is a truth as sure as the law of gravity itself?[2].

---

[2]   Sorko--Ram, Ari and Shira (1992 December) , Maoz Newsletter.

Furthermore, there is no lack of accounts from our own experiences that curses are real. We have successfully delivered many Christians from curses. We ourselves have been delivered from curses, which we will share in a subsequent chapter. When curses are canceled, blessings flow.

Every deliverance minister with whom we are acquainted, regularly deals with curses in the lives of Christians. If it is possible for a Christian to be under a curse, it is possible for a Christian to have a demon; for the power of a curse is demonic.

From our earliest days of casting out demons, we learned to deal with demons of curses. We did so before we fully understood curses and blessings from a scriptural viewpoint. The Holy Spirit would give us words of knowledge when we were casting demons out of people, and we would know by the Spirit that there were curses on them. In fact, it was this continual dealing with curses in people's lives that prompted us to do a Bible study on curses. We were amazed to discover how much the Bible says about curses and blessings.

For the sake of understanding curses, it is helpful to divide them into several logical categories: Generational Curses, Personal Sin Curses, Accursed Things, Word Curses, Founding Father Curses and Witchcraft Curses. First, we will consider Generational Curses.

2

GENERATIONAL CURSES

> I call heaven and earth to record this day against you, that I have set before you life and death, blessing and cursing: therefore choose life, THAT BOTH THOU AND THY SEED MAY LIVE.
>
> Deut. 30:19 (Emphasis ours)

When a man chooses to walk in obedience to God, he is assured of the blessings of God upon his life; and these blessings will pass down to his children and his children's children. Conversely, when a man chooses to ignore God's commandments, or openly rebels against God's laws, he will be cursed. Furthermore, the curse will pass down to his descendants.

> Thou shalt not make unto thee any graven image, or any likeness of any thing that is in heaven above, or that is in the earth beneath, or that is in the water under the earth: Thou shalt not bow down thyself to them, nor serve them: for I the Lord thy God am a jealous God, VISITING THE INIQUITY OF THE FATHERS UPON THE CHILDREN UNTO THE THIRD AND FOURTH GENERATION

OF THEM THAT HATE ME; AND
SHEWING MERCY UNTO THOUSANDS OF
THEM THAT LOVE ME, AND KEEP MY
COMMANDMENTS.

Exodus 20:4-6 (Emphasis ours)

God met with Moses on Mt. Sinai and gave him the Ten Commandments. In these commandments God forbad idolatry under the penalty of a curse that would pass down "unto the third and the fourth generation" Exodus 34:7. Suppose a man commits the sin of idolatry [which includes anything occult]. Further suppose that he and each of his descendants for four generations have three children each. This adds up to forty "seed" who will come under the curse of that one man's iniquity.

By going backward on the generational chart, each of us has two parents, four grandparents, eight great-grandparents and sixteen great-great grandparents -- a total of thirty ancestors from which curses have possibly derived. By looking at the cause for curses in this light, it is easy to see how one could be suffering all sorts of curses due to ancestral sins.

Who would have accurate knowledge of what particular idolatries his forefathers had committed in past generations? Therefore, how would one know what curses need to be broken? The Holy spirit often reveals the cause of ancestral curses by supernatural "words of knowledge."

When we were in pastoral ministry, we would schedule a Deliverance Day one day each month for people outside our local fellowship who wanted to come for deliverance. It astonished us to see how far some people would travel for just a few hours of teaching and ministry. At one of these

10

meetings, there was a particular lady who came from three hundred miles away -- a person we had never met before. During a time of group ministry, Ida Mae received a "word of knowledge" that this woman had a curse of mental illness due to a sin committed by her grandfather. We prayed for the woman to be set free from that particular curse.

Seven years later we learned the rest of the story. The day before that particular Deliverance Day, this lady had been furloughed from a mental hospital. She had been in and out of mental hospitals for years. When she returned home from our deliverance meeting, family and friends kept expecting her to relapse into mental illness again, just as she had for years, but she never did. From the day of her deliverance, she was completely healed of mental illness and is now a stable leader in the church where her husband is an elder. The ancestral curse had been broken!

Ancestral curses are more often determined by their ill effects. Deuteronomy, chapter twenty-eight, enumerates several common effects of curses that can be paraphrased as follows:

(1) Poverty or perpetual financial insufficiency
(2) Barrenness and impotency together with miscarriages and related female complications
(3) Failure. Plans and projects meet with disaster
(4) Untimely and unnatural deaths
(5) Sickness and diseases; especially chronic and hereditary diseases
(6) Life traumas; going from one crisis to another
(7) Mental and emotional breakdown
(8) Breakdown of family relationships, including divorce

(9) Spiritually hindered in hearing God's voice,
sensing God's presence, understanding the
Bible, concentration in prayer and being
devoid of spiritual gifts.

Throughout Bible history the Jews witnessed the operation of generational curses. As we have already noted, they devised a proverb to describe the effects of a father's sin being passed down. They said, "The fathers have eaten sour grapes, and the children's teeth are set on edge" Ezekiel 18:2. However, God declared that the time would come when this proverb would no longer be appropriate. His people would come under "a new covenant". He would write His law "in their hearts," and every man would become directly responsible for his own sins. (See: Jer. 31:29-33; Ezek. 18:1-4). This new covenant is the covenant of grace that Jesus provided through the shedding of His precious blood.

Grace does not mean that a curse can no longer alight and pass down through the generations. Grace means that, through the substitutionary death of Jesus, God has provided a remedy for the curse.

Christ hath redeemed us from the curse of the
law, being made a curse for us: for it is written,
Cursed is every one that hangeth on a tree.
Galatians 3:13

Anyone who has evidence of generational curses operating in his life should appropriate the provisions of the cross. Let him confess his own sins and the sins (known and unknown) of his forefathers. The effects of curses are merely the works of the devil which Jesus came to destroy (I John

3:8). The demons that perpetuate curses can now be driven out. They must be commanded to go in the name of Jesus!

The very first time that we taught on curses, a fourteen-year-old boy was delivered of a generational curse and was dramatically healed. The mother brought this young man to the altar for prayer. She explained that the boy was born totally deaf. He had never heard sound; therefore, he was also mute. Ida Mae received a word of knowledge that this deafness was a curse due to the mother's involvement in fortune telling. The mother admitted that subsequent to giving her heart to the Lord she was much involved in fortune telling. First, we led the mother to repent and ministered deliverance to the mother.

Then, we prayed for the boy. We charged the demon of curse that he no longer had any legal right to the boy. When the demon was cast out, the boy instantly received his hearing. Someone began to play a praise tape over the church's speaker system. The young fellow was grinning from ear to ear and nodding his head to the rhythm of the music. It was his first time to hear music.

The next morning the mother called the church office. She said, "I just wanted you to know that my son is still healed. He can hear perfectly." This call was certainly a confirmation to us that the teaching on curses was right on target.

3

PERSONAL SIN CURSES

Many of God's people are struggling against adversities and evils in their lives, not recognizing that their problems are due to sin curses. Curses come in through the "Sin Door".

CURSED IS THE MAN WHO DOES NOT UPHOLD THE WORDS OF THIS LAW BY CARRYING THEM OUT.
> Deut. 27:26 (New International Version)
(Emphasis ours)

Sin is disobedience to God's commandments. In God's sight, partial obedience is disobedience. King Saul is an example. God commissioned Saul to destroy the Amalekites who came against the Israelites who were coming out of the wilderness into their Canaan inheritance. God had pronounced a judgment curse upon the Amalekites: "I will utterly put out the remembrance of Amalek from under heaven" Exod. 17:14.

Years later, the judgment of Amalek was finally ripe, so God instructed Saul to completely destroy the Amalekites.[3] He was not to spare man, woman, child or livestock. Everything pertaining to the Amalekites was devoted to destruction. However, Saul spared King Agag and the best of

---

[3]   See: I Samuel 15

14

the sheep, oxen, and the fat calves and lambs. Saul's partial obedience was judged to be rebellion -- even as the sin of witchcraft. Because of this disobedience God rejected Saul from being king. Failure, or refusal, to obey God's commandments brings a curse. If we expect to stay free of sin curses, we must walk in obedience to God.

How can one know if he is under a sin curse? First of all, has one despised God, or refused to hearken to His voice? God's blessings come to those who are doers of His Word. Curses come upon all who "will not hearken unto the voice of the Lord thy God, to observe to do all his commandments and his statutes" Deut. 28:15.

The Bible specifically names many sins which result in curses; for example:

1. Idolatry. (Either making or worshipping an idol.) Deut. 27:15; Exod. 20:5
2. Dishonoring one's parents. Deut. 27:16
3. Defrauding one's neighbor. Deut. 27:17
4. Cruelty to a handicapped person. Deut. 27:17
5. Oppressing the defenseless. Deut. 27:19
6. Fornication. Deut. 22:21-29
7. Incest with one's sister, mother-in law or father's wife. Deut. 27:29,22,23
8. Sexual relationship with any animal. Deut. 27:21
9. Adultery. Deut. 22:22-27; Job. 24:15-18; Num. 5:27; Lev. 20:10
10. Homosexual relationships. Lev. 20:13; Gen. 19:13,24,25
11. Sexual intercourse during menstruation. Lev. 20:13
12. Marrying a woman & her mother. Lev. 20:14
13. Rape. Deut. 22:25
14. Children conceived out of wedlock. Deut. 23:2

15. Accursed objects in one's possession..
    Deut. 7:25,26
16. Any occult practice (divination, sorcery, omens, witchcraft, consulting a medium, consulting the dead). Deut. 18:9-13. Lev. 20:6, 27
17. Murder. Deut. 27:24
18. Murder for hire. (Including those who are paid to perform abortions) Deut. 27:25
19. Forsaking the Lord. Deut. 28:20
20. Not serving the Lord joyfully and gladly in the time of prosperity. Deut. 28:46
21. Not reverencing the name of the Lord God. Deut. 28:58
22. Presumption in thinking that one can disregard God's Word and devise his own way. Deut. 29:19
23. Cursing or mistreating Abraham's seed. Gen. 12:3; 27:29; Num.24:9
24. Refusing to help in the Lord's warfare. Jud. 5:23; Jer. 48:10b
25. Failure to give God the glory. Mal. 2:2
26. Robbing God of tithes and offerings. Mal. 3:9; Hag.1:6-9
27. Neglecting the work of the Lord. Jer. 48:10a
28. Enticing others away from the Lord into a false religion. Deut. 13:18-21
29. Taking away or adding to the Word of God. Rev. 22:18-19
30. Teaching rebellion against the Lord. Jer. 28:16-17
31. Refusing to warn those who sin. Ezek. 3:18-21
32. Defiling the Sabbath. Exod. 31:14; Num.15:32-36
33. Perversion of the Gospel of Christ. Gal. 1:8-9.
34. Cursing one's rulers. I Kgs. 2:8-9; Exod. 22:28

35. Refusal to forgive others after asking God to forgive you. Matt. 18:34,35
36. Child sacrifice (Example: abortion). Deut. 18:10; Lev. 18:21
37. Disobedience against any of the Lord's commandments. Deut. 11:28; 27:26

There is yet another way to determine whether or not one is under a curse: by comparing his life to the blessings God has promised to those who love Him. If one is not blessed, he is cursed. How does your life measure up to the blessings enumerated in Deuteronomy 28:1-14? Are you "set on high" by God, a lender and not a borrower, the head and not the tail? Is your life characterized by fruitfulness? Do you prosper -- coming and going? Are you free from the harassment of enemies -- both natural and spiritual? Is your life a success? Is your relationship with God gratifying; are you recognizing and fulfilling His purposes? These are the earmarks of a blessed life. If one is not enjoying the blessing, then he is suffering the curse. There is no in-between.

Yet another way to determine if curses are in operation is to look for the effects of curses. Common effects of curses are poverty, barrenness, pestilence, chronic sickness, failure, defeat, humiliation, insanity, torment, perpetual traumas, spiritual hindrances, domination by others and abandonment by God and others. (See: Deuteronomy 28:20-68).

In 1979 we made our first overseas ministry trip. As we prepared for the work ahead, we wondered if we would find the same demons in other countries that we had found in the United States. It didn't take long to discover that demons are the same the world over.

17

Church leaders brought a man to us for help. He was mentally ill. He had been in this condition for ten years and was unable to support his wife and three children. The burden was heavy on the family. Through a "word of knowledge" we knew that this man's mental problem was due to a sin curse. He had committed some sin for which he was carrying a heavy guilt, and the guilt had actually driven him crazy.

We confronted the brother with this "word of knowledge", but he was embarrassed to tell us what he had done. After much loving persuasion he finally confided in us that as a young man, being raised on a farm, he had committed the sin of bestiality with some of the farm animals.

He was sure that he had committed the unpardonable sin and that it was useless to confess his sin to God. We were having to work through an interpreter, but we finally put it across that God would forgive him if he would repent and ask God's pardon. We led him in a confession prayer and cast out the demons of curse.

By the next day, his wife knew that he was truly delivered. She said, "He is like a bird out of a cage. He doesn't realize yet that he is free." Months later, we received a letter from the man. He was no longer mentally ill; he had gone back to work soon after we had prayed for him.

Two years later, we were back in that country. When the man who had been delivered from the curse of mental illness (brought on by the sin of bestiality) heard that we were in the country, he sent for us to come to his home for a special thanksgiving dinner. We celebrated his deliverance with family and friends and gave praise to Jesus, our Deliverer.

Eleven years later, we received a letter from this dear brother. He once again wrote to thank us that we allowed

God to use us in his behalf. His testimony had just been published in his denomination's magazine.

In Deuteronomy 27, idolatry is the first sin mentioned that brings a curse. God looks upon idolatry as spiritual adultery. The reason that God gives for extending a curse to the third and fourth generation is: "I the Lord thy God am a JEALOUS God" Exod. 20:5. Those who divide their loyalty or seek another god are said to "hate" the Lord.

If one goes outside the marriage relationship to get his or her sexual needs met, he or she has committed adultery. Idolatry is spiritual adultery because all of our needs are to be met by our Husband God. Idolatry is going to a provider other than God for wisdom, guidance, favor or power. As we mentioned earlier, the occult is idolatry. Fortune telling, witchcraft, sorcery, divination, necromancy and astrology are forbidden fruit. Remember what God said to Eve about forbidden fruit: "Ye shall not eat of it, neither shall ye TOUCH it, lest ye die" Genesis 3:3, (Emphasis ours).

It only takes a "touch" with the occult to snare a person and bring on a curse. Frank tells how he learned this lesson the hard way.

For the first twenty years of my pastoral ministry, I struggled under the effects of a curse. Whenever I read the Bible, my mind was severely bound. It was a struggle to get anything out of the Word of God. I was ignorant of curses all those years and had no inkling as to the cause for this mind-binding problem. Finally, when I became involved in deliverance ministry, I began to understand the workings of curses, and God revealed to me the source of my problem.

While a student at Southwestern Baptist Theological Seminary in Ft. Worth, Texas, I took a course on cults. My professor instructed me to visit five cult meetings, observe what took place and write a term paper based on my experiences. I visited a spiritualist meeting where the man presiding was a medium. He purported to receive information from the spirit of a deceased uncle. The man was what the Bible calls a "necromancer", one who inquires of the dead. Of course, it is impossible to contact a dead person. The medium actually contacts a familiar spirit -- a spirit familiar with the medium and familiar with the deceased person. The familiar spirit sometimes appears as a particular dead person and may mimic the deceased person's voice.

I had "touched" the occult realm. I was snared. I was spiritually crippled. Twenty years later, when God showed me the root, I promptly repented of going to the spiritualist meeting, forgave the professor who had required it of me, and had Ida Mae cast out the demon of curse. I was immediately, completely and permanently set free. The chain upon my mind was broken!

Seventy percent of the people in the deliverance conferences that we conduct admit to spiritual hindrances. They are hindered in prayer life, Bible study, hearing God's voice, worship, praise, gifts of the Holy Spirit and ministry unto the Lord. In digging for root causes to these hindrances, we have discovered that the vast majority have had some contact with the occult; and this is the key to their getting set free.

The occult is just another term for idolatry: going to a source other than God to satisfy one's desires. Psalm 115 tells us exactly what happens when we become idolaters: "They that make them [idols] are like unto them; so is every one that trusteth in them" Ps. 115:8.

The idolator becomes like the idol! How is that? Idols have mouths but cannot speak. When a person is prayed for to receive the baptism in the Holy Spirit and is unable to speak in tongues, the root cause is usually involvement in the occult.

Idols have eyes but cannot see. The idolater is spiritually blinded. He cannot perceive spiritual things.

Idols have ears, but they hear not. Many Christians are unable to hear the voice of God. They are hindered because of their dealings with idols.

Idols have noses, yet they are unable to smell. The Bible says that Christ, our beloved Bridegroom, is "perfumed with myrrh and frankincense, with all powders of the merchant" The Song of Solomon 3:6. Those who have trafficked in idols cannot sense the Lord's fragrance. They are unaware of His presence.

Demons are sometimes discerned through smell. The Bible calls them " unclean spirits", and they have a very offensive odor.

Unclean spirits sometimes cause people to be unclean and neglect personal hygiene. Such people do not realize that they are filthy.

We met Scout in Aspen, Colorado. He was a dirty Hippie -- with long matted hair -- whom we led to Christ while ministering deliverance to one of his friends. It was a very cold evening there in the mountains, and Scout was wearing a leather coat similar to the kind worn by the frontiersmen. He carried a Bowie knife on his belt.

As we knelt together, we led Scout into the baptism of the Holy Spirit. As he prayed in tongues, demons began to come out of him. He couldn't understand what was happening to him, but we quietly continued to command demons to come out of him.

It was getting warm in the old Community Church building where we were ministering, and Scout took off his coat. We saw that he was wearing an occult necklace, and we asked him to remove it. He kept taking off layers of clothing until he was down to his thermal undershirt. His underclothing was filthy. He obviously had not had a bath in months. Suddenly he became aware of his uncleanness. He began to smell himself. As he ran his fingertips over his dirty undershirt he uttered in amazement, "I am so dirty!" As he was filled with the purity of God, he became aware of his filthiness.

For years afterward Scout wrote to us on the anniversary of his new birth experience. The last time that we heard from him, he was still following the Lord and was ministering with a Pentecostal evangelist in Florida.

Idols have hands, but they cannot handle. One's hands represent one's ministry. Hands that cannot "handle" are hindered in ministry.

Idols have feet, but they cannot walk. One's feet and walk speak of one's ability to minister; like the beautiful feet that bear the Gospel (See: Isa. 52:7; Rom. 10:15). The idolater is crippled in his ministry.

Idols cannot speak through their throats. Those who make idols or trust in them are hindered in their witness. Their speech is bound.

Spiritual hindrance is a curse. How glorious it is to be liberated from the bondage of idolatry!

4

ACCURSED THINGS

The graven images of their gods you shall burn
with fire; you shall not desire the silver or gold
that is on them, nor take it [the silver or gold]
for yourself, lest you be ensnared by it; for it is
an abomination to the Lord your God. Neither
shall you bring an abomination (an idol) into
your house, LEST YOU BECOME AN
ACCURSED THING LIKE IT; but you shall
utterly detest and abhor it, for it is an accursed
thing.
Deut. 7:25,26 *Amplified*, (Brackets and
emphasis ours)

One comes under a curse when he takes an accursed
thing into his possession. The Hebrew word for "accursed
thing" is *cherem;* literally, "devoted thing." Things that are
devoted to God become curses to the person who takes those
things for himself.
Jericho was the first-fruits of the conquest of Canaan.
The spoils of the city were a tithe unto the Lord.

And the city shall be accursed [devoted], even
it, and all that are therein, to the Lord...And ye,
in any wise keep yourselves from the accursed

[devoted] thing, lest ye make yourselves accursed, when ye take of the accursed [devoted] thing, and make the camp of Israel a curse, and trouble it. But all the silver, and gold, and vessels of brass and iron, are consecrated unto the Lord: they shall come into the treasury of the Lord.

Joshua 7:17-19, (Brackets = marginal reading)

Achan took a robe, some gold and some silver: things devoted to God. He robbed God, and what he took became a curse to him, his family and to all the camp of Israel. Because of Achan's sin, Israel's enemies were able to smite them. In order to remove the curse, Achan, his family, and his total possessions were destroyed. This was the penalty under the law of Moses.

Likewise, if we take for ourselves what is devoted to God we, too, become cursed. A curse of poverty cannot be broken if one is withholding God's tithe.

Will a man rob God? Yet ye have robbed me. But ye say, Wherein have we robbed thee? In tithes and offerings. Ye are CURSED WITH A CURSE: for ye have robbed me, even this whole nation.

Malachi 3:8,9 (Emphasis ours)

Furthermore, idolatrous or occult objects in one's possession bring a curse. God has decreed that all such objects are devoted for destruction.

Herbert[4] invited us to his home for dinner. It was to be an opportunity for us to minster to his fourteen-year-old son who was awakened every night by frightening dreams.

Herbert worked for the Assemblies of God denomination, filming missionaries on their fields of ministry. His work had taken him to several African countries. We discovered his home was decorated with witchcraft paraphernalia given to him by missionaries. For example, on one wall were a real witch's mask and a witch doctor's fetish made from a cow's tail. On a shelf was a collection of small figures of men involved in perverted sex.

The demonic atmosphere in the home was stifling. No wonder their son had nightmares! However, Herbert defended his prized objects of witchcraft. He valued them and refused our advice to destroy them. We were unable to help their son.

Years later, Herbert attended a conference where we were teaching. He reported that after we left he decided that our counsel was right. He had destroyed all the witchcraft artifacts and cleansed the house of demons. His son was then able to sleep peacefully.

There are many things classified as "art" that have demons associated with them. In Acts we learn of certain new converts who had to do some serious house cleaning. This is a pattern for us to heed.

> And many that believed came, and confessed,
> and shewed their deeds. Many of them also
> which used CURIOUS ARTS brought their

---

[4]   Names of persons used in illustrations have been changed throughout the book.

books together, and burned them before all men; and they counted the price of them, and found it fifty thousand pieces of silver.

Acts 19:19 (Emphasis ours)

"Curious arts" refers to arts that "pry into forbidden things, with the aid of evil spirits."[5] Demonic art carries an air of strangeness that evokes curiosity; hence, curious art. We need to take stock of curious arts in our possession. Curio shops specialize in curious arts. When one buys a curio, he usually gets a bonus -- a demon spirit!

We had been ministering intently for five days. We were ready for a break. Our friends, the Hendersons, invited us to their lovely home for breakfast. It promised to be a leisurely time when we could relax from spiritual warfare and see no demon, hear no demon and speak no demon.

After breakfast we went into the den and sank into comfortable chairs. On the coffee table in front of Ida Mae was an artistic vase. The Holy Spirit began to show Ida what the vase represented. She did not want to see it. She tried to ignore what the Holy Spirit was saying. After all, we were there just to relax and visit.

It was as though the Holy Spirit took His finger and drew an outline of what the vase portrayed. It was a replica of the female reproductive organs. Reluctantly, Ida yielded to the Holy Spirit's prompting and said, "Maggie, I've got to show you what this vase represents. It's perverted art." As Ida traced the outline of the vase with her finger, she explained,

---

[5]   Vine, W. E. (1952). Vine's Expository Dictionary of New Testament Words. Iowa Falls, Iowa: Riverside Book & Bible House, p. 253.

"The base is the vagina followed by the uterus. Here are the Fallopian tubes and the ovaries."

Maggie, sprang from her chair, grabbed the vase, ran to the door and threw the vase outside. The three of us were startled at Maggie's strong reaction.

Then, Maggie explained. While her husband was in military service, they had traveled to various countries. When he was stationed in Italy, they purchased the vase because it was Venetian glass, unique to Italy. It was a joke between them that although they had moved many times, and many things got broken, the delicate vase never was broken.

As Ida Mae explained what the Holy Spirit revealed about the vase, Maggie had suddenly realized that major physical problems had begun in her female organs from the time they purchased the vase. Eventually, they had to return to the United States because of her female problems. She had a hysterectomy that revealed clusters of tumors inside and outside her uterus. As we prayed deliverance for Maggie, Ida began to speak by the Holy Spirit's guidance to "roots" that had gone down from Maggie's female organs into her legs. Maggie confirmed that this was true. Her legs were bothering her to such an extent that she had taken up running to try to alleviate the pain.

The Holy Spirit instructed the Hendersons to destroy the vase and remove the pieces from their property lest their land be polluted. They carried every sliver of the broken glass to the county dump.

We urge that people be cautious about collecting souvenirs and mementos when visiting countries and areas where witchcraft and idolatry are prevalent. For example, the American Indians of the southwestern United States are known to perform ceremonies in association with artistry they offer for sale. Turquoise jewelry, the woven *ojo* (God's Eye) and woven wall hangings are commonly defiled. Flaws are woven into tapestries as openings to receive spirits.

The colorful strings of red chili peppers are offerings to a heathen god. "The Aztecs so revered and respected the chili that they deified the plant as a minor war god."[6]

Frank relates the following encounter that he had with a missionary evangelist we will call Philip.

Philip had heard a radio announcement of our deliverance seminar. His theological persuasion was that a Christian cannot have a demon. Yet, the Holy Spirit pressed upon him that if he would come to the meeting he would be healed. He had come early, so I took him into the Pastor's study for prayer.

Philip identified himself as a missionary evangelist. He was on crutches, having seriously injured his ankle and foot by a fall from a ladder. He had been through surgery and six weeks in a cast. Intense pain persisted, and the doctors were of the opinion that he would always be crippled.

Subsequent to the foot injury, he had also been involved in a private plane crash from which he miraculously survived. The more he shared, the more I was certain that Philip was under a curse. Then the key information came to light.

While on an evangelistic mission to Haiti, Philip had been invited to a Voodoo meeting. Although other missionaries counseled him that it was dangerous to go, he was curious to gather first hand information on their occult practices. In the midst of the Voodoo ritual; a man, under the influence of demons, began to eat a thick, glass tumbler. He

---

[6]   Bowman, J. (Fall 1992). Heart and Soul Food. Friendly Exchange Magazine, p. 13.

offered Philip the uneaten portion as a souvenir. Philip had also taken pictures of the rituals to show people wherever he preached.

I explained that the half-eaten tumbler and the pictures must be destroyed. His attendance at the Voodoo ceremony, plus the possession of the glass and pictures, had certainly put him under a curse. Philip agreed to destroy them as soon as he returned home. I then led him in a prayer of repentance, renunciation of the occult and calling upon the Lord for deliverance. "You spirit of Voodoo," I commanded, "Come out of him!" Philip exploded into coughing and, within seconds, jumped to his feet, leaping and praising God. He was completely healed!

Philip left his crutches in the pastor's office, and, at the end of the service, stood with me to minister healing and deliverance to the people.

There is also much so-called "Christian art" that violates God's commandment: "You shall not MAKE for yourself an idol in the form of anything in heaven above or on the earth beneath or in the waters below" Exod. 20:4 (Emphasis ours).

When pictures and statuary are created as representations of The Father, Son or Holy Spirit, they are idols. They are an abomination to God because God is incorruptible, and He cannot be represented by anything that is corruptible.

> Professing themselves to be wise, they became fools, And CHANGED THE GLORY OF THE UNCORRUPTIBLE GOD into an image made like to corruptible man, and to birds, and fourfooted beasts, and creeping things.
> Romans 1:23 (Emphasis ours)

When an image of a dove is made to represent the Holy Spirit, or an artist's concept of Jesus is made to represent the Son of God, is this not a violation of the commandment not to make any likeness of the Godhead? Further, such objects become occult amulets when kept, worn or carried to bring good luck or to protect a person from harm. Even the symbol of the cross can be corrupted in this way.

We taught on Christian idolatry at a camp whose book store sold little, silver Christian symbols. When a certain person who heard our teaching attempted to return his dove for a refund, it set off a furor. The camp authorities reacted as had the silversmiths at Ephesus who "made silver shrines for [the goddess] Diana" that "brought no small gain unto the craftsmen." Why was Demetrius so upset? He said to the silversmiths, "Sirs, ye know that by this craft we have our wealth" (See: Acts 19:23-41).

Not too many years ago fundamental Christians condemned Roman Catholics for their icons and considered any image representing the Godhead to be reprehensible. Now, however, such statues and pictures are sanctioned and sought after. Today, we find most Christian book stores ladened with idolatrous artifacts. "Christian" idolatry may be rationalized and defended, but this does not overthrow Scripture nor enable one to escape the curse associated with it.

A so-called "Jesus picture" is not a picture of Jesus. It is actually the picture of "another Jesus".

The Holy Spirit will teach those who are teachable, and when one continues in God's Word he will be a true disciple to whom truth is revealed.

The following testimony is given by a dear friend, Evelyn Marzullo:

30

As I began to study the scriptures more intensely, the Lord opened up a revelation to me concerning idolatry and how easily it can enter our lives.

There was a beautiful picture of Jesus hanging on my dining room wall. The picture showed Jesus so gentle and with a tender smile on His face. Often during the course of the day, I walked past this picture, but couldn't pass it without stopping to stare and pray for awhile. One day while gazing upon it, I heard these words in my mind: "If you keep looking at this picture, you won't know Me when you see Me." That was a frightening thought. I didn't realize that this picture had become too important to me, for it was the only way I saw Jesus.

I took the picture down immediately and destroyed it, knowing that in doing so I was being obedient to the Lord.[7]

We do not expose Christian idolatry because it is a popular word and received with great enthusiasm, but we are compelled to be faithful to God and His Word and to teaching truth to God's people. Jesus declared, "Ye shall know the truth and the truth shall make you free" John 8:32. Deliverance is in relationship to truth; it is in proportion to truth embraced.

When Jesus taught, "Whoso eateth my flesh, and drinketh my blood, hath eternal life" John 6:54, His disciples complained that it was a "hard saying" and "from that time

---

[7]   Marzullo, E. (1993). He Said, "Follow Me", p.22..

31

many of his disciples went back, and walked no more with him" John 6:65.

Most Christians readily affirm a desire to hear truth, but some truth is "a hard saying": hard to bear and falls on stony ground.

The Word of the Lord to the church today is comparable to the Word of the Lord that came to Ezekiel: "Son of man, cause Jerusalem to know her abominations" Ezek. 16:2. Ezekiel had the unthankful duty of informing the people of God of their idolatrous abominations. Today, God's spokesmen must be equally faithful in exposing idolatry within the church.

In the midst of a one-on-one deliverance with Betty Sue, she puzzled us with a very strange question: "Why does Jesus hate me?" We assured her that Jesus loved her; He died on the cross for her. "Why do you say that Jesus hates you?" we probed. "Because I have a picture of Jesus over my bed," she explained, "and every night while I'm sleeping He comes down out of the picture and beats me."

It was not the Lord Jesus Christ who attacked Betty Sue; it was the spirit of "another Jesus". Through venerating the picture, she had received "another spirit" -- the false Jesus and the wrong spirit that Paul warned about in II Corinthians 11:4.

There is not one hint in all of scripture as to Jesus' physical appearance. God in His wisdom knows that man is prone to make images. Besides, God intends that we remember our Lord in His glorification rather than in His humiliation.

> [No] even though we once did estimate Christ
> from a human viewpoint and as a man, yet now

[we have such knowledge of Him that] we know
Him no longer [in terms of the flesh].
                    II Cor. 4:16b, (Amplified)

Have you ever seen an ugly portrayal of Jesus? Most artists depict him as very handsome, yet Isaiah prophesied of our Savior, "He had no beauty or majesty to attract us to him, nothing in his appearance that we should desire him" Isaiah 53:2b, NIV.

How are we to remember Jesus? Jesus has told us how we are to remember Him. We are to remember Him through the symbols of the Lord's Supper: the broken bread that represents his broken body and the wine that speaks to us of His shed blood. "This do in remembrance of me" I Cor. 11:24,25. Yet, it is not the dead Christ Whom we are to remember, but the Person Who died for us; "an affectionate calling of the Person Himself to mind."[8]

If the Shroud of Turin had proved to be authentic, imagine the flood of idolatry that would have been loosed upon the church?

Ida Mae recalls a young Presbyterian lady who experienced intense pain in her head during our teaching. Our attention was drawn to the wooden crucifix worn about her neck. The Spirit of God revealed to us that this was the cause of her pain. The demons of pain and suffering, associated with the crucifix, had become excited because of our teaching and had manifested themselves.

We asked the lady why she, a Presbyterian, would be wearing a crucifix. She explained that it had been given to

---

[8]   Vine, W. E. (1952). Expository Dictionary of New Testament Words, Riverside Book & Bible House, p. 946-947.

her by an aunt. It had belonged to her grandmother and was a family heirloom. She refused our counsel to remove the crucifix and left the service still in pain.

A crucifix presents a dead Christ. It is a symbol of suffering and shame, and attracts those sorts of spirits to the one who wears one. It is a *memento mori*: a death's head and a reminder of death. A more appropriate symbol would be an empty tomb. Our Redeemer lives; and, because He lives, we live also!

Doris, a sweet Christian lady, invited us to her home for a visit while we were teaching in her city. She specifically requested that we go through her house to determine if there were any objects that would attract evil spirits. She also wanted us to pray for her eyes; she was losing her vision.

On a shelf in her living room was a sculptured bust, obviously representing Jesus in the agony of death. Blood was running down the face from the crown of thorns, the eyes were rolled back in the head and tears flowed down the cheek: a true *memento mori*. It was gruesome! We said, "Doris, you need to get rid of this image. This is what the Bible calls 'another Jesus'. It is idolatrous."

Doris explained that each day she would stand in front of the image, look into its eyes and that tears would run down her own cheeks.

"Doris, the Lord is showing us why you are losing your eye sight. It is the image. It is your looking into the eyes of the image that has harmed you. This is not Jesus."

"But my best friend gave it to me," countered Doris. "If I destroyed it, Henry wouldn't understand."

We knew Henry: a fine man. We assured her that Henry would understand.

Doris couldn't decide what to do. She seemed convinced that the image needed to be destroyed, but she was fearful of offending Henry. She didn't make her decision that day. Perhaps she did the right thing, later. We pray that she was delivered of the curse of idolatry and that her eyes were healed.

It is sad that some people choose the curse and refuse the blessing. It is easy to be captured by the value of an accursed object or to be bound by a sentimental attachment.

Jesus has taught us that those who follow Him must count the cost. How determined are we to obey the Lord? Having to give up material possessions as a condition to deliverance from curses will surely test one's sincerity.

5

WORD CURSES

Life's problems are like trees: they have roots. More and more often we are discovering problems rooted in curses: curses from the sins of our forefathers, curses from one's personal transgressions of God's commandments, witchcraft curses and curses generated by spoken evil.

"Death and life are in the power of the tongue" Prov. 18:21. Spoken words have power either to bless or curse. Jesus said to a fig tree: "No man eat fruit of thee hereafter for ever" Mark 11:14, and by the next morning the tree had withered from the roots. On another occasion Jesus uttered the words, "Lazurus, come forth" John 11:43, and a man who had been dead for four days walked out of his tomb. The power of death and life were in His tongue. Death and life are also in the power of our tongues. Whenever we speak we minister: either to curse or to bless, to tear down or to build up.

Speech is a lighted match. It can be used to light the lamp of Christian witness, or to start a forest fire of destruction.

> The tongue...is a fire, a world of evil among the parts of the body. It corrupts the whole person, sets the whole course of his life on fire, AND IS

ITSELF SET ON FIRE BY HELL...out of the
same mouth proceedeth blessing and cursing.
My brethren, these things ought not to be.

James 3:6-10, NIV (Emphasis ours)

When dealing with word curses we must consider:
(1) Evil words that others have spoken against us.
(2) Evil words that we have spoken against others.
(3) Evil words that we have spoken against ourselves.

When We Speak Evil Against Others

Evil words can produce curses, not only when they are
spoken maliciously, but also when spoken carelessly. This is
why it is so very important that we learn to discipline our
tongues, on the one hand, and, on the other hand, break the
power of words that speak ill of us.

When we speak evil of others, we curse them. The Word
of God commands us to "bless and curse not" Romans 12;14.
Therefore, cursing others brings a curse upon oneself.
Disobedience to God's command not to curse others will bring
a curse (See: Deut. 27:26).

It concerns us that some teachers are said to advocate
cursing others and returning a curse upon the one who curses
you. Jesus taught otherwise:

But I say unto you, Love your enemies, BLESS
THEM THAT CURSE YOU, do good to them
that hate you, and pray for them which
despitefully use you, and persecute you.

Matt. 5:44 (Emphasis ours)

It is sobering, to say the least, that each of us will give an account of our words on the day of judgment.

> But I say unto you, That every idle word that
> men shall speak, they shall give account thereof
> in the day of judgment.
>
> Matt. 12:36

Agros, the Greek word for "idle", signifies words that are fruitless, unprofitable or barren. Peter uses the word to express ineffectiveness; that is, words without corresponding works of faith; hence, worthless or unfruitful words (See: II Pet. 1:8)

Which of us has not spoken things that we wish we could "un-speak?" Words once spoken are beyond recall. We are left with only one recourse: to "overcome evil with good" by blessing those whom we have formerly cursed. It would be profitable to pause right now and bless anyone whom you have ever cursed.

Too often cursing of others takes place within families. Parents curse their children with such words as, "You're no good; you'll never amount to anything; you're stupid", or similar references. Such children grow up to be failures, who never succeed in life, because of the negative confessions made over them by their parents. They are cursed children.

Children curse parents when they express dishonor and disrespect by disdain, impudence, sassiness and back-talk.

Husbands and wives curse one another when they belittle, criticize and condemn one another instead of showing mutual love and respect. Husbands and wives should realize that they have become "one flesh". To speak evil of one's spouse is to speak evil of oneself. Marriage ties are weakened, and curses are imposed when a spouse speaks evil of his or her companion. It is inconsistent that the fountain within "send forth at the same place sweet water and bitter" James 3:11. A pastor, for example, is a hypocrite if he speaks words of life in church but spews out curses and death upon his family at home.

When Others Speak Evil Against Us

Suppose someone has spoken, or continues to speak, evil of us, of which we are not aware. Are we responsible to routinely extricate ourselves from unknown curses? If we follow this line of thinking, we will quickly become paranoid; being controlled by a fear that others are secretly plotting or practicing evil against us.

It is important that we understand a basic biblical principle. Demons cannot enter at will; they must have a legal right, or a gateway of opportunity. Also, demons are the enforcers of a curse. Therefore, no one can put a curse (a demon) on us unless there is an opening in our own lives. "Like a fluttering sparrow or a darting swallow, an undeserved curse does not come to rest" Prov. 26:2,NIV.

When God's conditions have been met, a demon has no right to stay. He readily can be cast out in the Name of Jesus.

King Balak, the Moabite, sought out the prophet, Balaam, to put a curse on Israel. Balak had seen what Israel's armies had done to the Amorites, and he sought to protect himself through witchcraft. Even though Balaam wanted the reward that King Balak offered him, Balaam was unable to put a curse upon God's people. He lamented, "How can I curse those whom God has not cursed?" Num. 23:8, NIV.

Praise God! Whoever is blessed by God cannot be cursed by the powers of witchcraft.

Our protection is not found in denouncing every supposed curse that others might have spoken against us, but our protection is in walking righteously before the Lord. Balaam could not curse Israel because the nation was walking in obedience to God. There was no cause -- no grounds -- for a curse to alight. When we have on the whole armor of God, we are protected from all evil that men would plot against us. We must continually be girded with truth, righteousness, faith, the Word of God, hope of salvation and a readiness to proclaim the gospel of peace. Spiritual diligence and discipline is required to put on each piece of armor.

Suppose one hears others speak evil against him, or hears through a third person that others have uttered curses against him -- what should he do? Does one then have a responsibility to denounce those words? One explanation may be the following:

Our ministry finances were not flowing, and we could not put a finger on the problem. We were in contact with two other deliverance ministries and learned that they, too, were in financial slumps. As we all talked and prayed together about our situations, the Lord reminded us of a certain person, about whom we had reliable information, that had spoken curses and prayed prayers against our ministries. The Holy Spirit reminded us that we had books in our libraries that were given to us by the one who had spoken evil of us. These books were points of contact for witchcraft curses to operate against our respective ministries.

We were led to do several things: destroy the books, express our forgiveness of that individual, ask the Lord to bless him, and, finally, to declare the curse broken. We confessed the blessings of God and commanded that, in the name of Jesus, every demon of curse get off our finances. Within a few weeks all three ministries were once again enjoying financial blessings.

Numbers, chapter thirty, gives laws concerning vows. The husband and father in a household is charged with taking definite action in regard to vows uttered by his wife or unmarried daughters. If the husband and father, the head of the family, hears any foolish vows; he can release the women by forbidding the vow to stand. However, if the husband and father says nothing, the vow stands and the wife or daughter is bound by her words.

This passage lays down a spiritual principle. The one in spiritual authority must rule over whatever is spoken within the family. He has authority to nullify foolish things spoken. By neglecting to use his authority, he permits the words to retain their power.

Evil words will stand when unchallenged. Therefore, when we know that curses have been spoken against us, we have the responsibility to disallow those evil words and break their power. Frank experienced the following:

It was the last night of a deliverance conference in Philadelphia, Pennsylvania. The praise service was in progress, and I was sitting on the front row. The Holy Spirit spoke to me, "There is about to be a confrontation." Just as I turned my head to look around, a man stepped in front of me. He declared, "I have a message from the Lord for you. You are a false prophet, and God is judging you. You will die and go to hell." I had been forewarned by the Holy Spirit. While the man was yet speaking, I began to renounce his words. Moving my arm like a baseball player calling out a base runner, I asserted, "You are not of God. I do not accept what

ʲu are saying. I break the power of your words." The man
.bruptly turned and walked away. I watched as he rejoined a
woman who had accompanied him, and the two quickly left
the meeting place. We later learned that this man and his
wife had done the same thing to other visiting ministers in
Philadelphia. My decisive action to break the power of evil
words spoken against me is an example of how one must take
definite authority over evil words spoken against him.

Ida Mae had an experience of her own which occurred
soon after a time of spiritual renewal when we were learning
to hear and heed the Holy Spirit's promptings. Ida Mae
recalls:

I was publicly attacked through a confrontation where
evil words were spoken against me. The Spirit had prepared
me ahead of time, although I did not realize it.

All one day I was pressed by the Spirit to read and
re-read Acts, chapter twenty-eight, verses one through
sixteen. This passage tells about Paul's shipwreck. He and
those with him were brought safely to land. It was cold and
raining, and the natives built a fire for them. These words
stood out:

**When Paul had gathered a bundle of sticks
and laid them on the fire, a viper came out
because of the heat, and fastened on his hand.**
v. 3.

The Lord kept telling me that the sticks, being wood,
represent the flesh of man. The fire speaks of God's
judgment. The heat of the fire (The Holy Spirit's anointing)
caused the viper (demon powers) to come forth (from man's
flesh) and fasten itself on Paul's hand (his ministry). When

the natives saw the viper hanging from Paul's hand, they doubted his integrity. However, Paul validated his ministry when he shook the creature off into the fire and suffered no harm.

That evening, to my surprise, the Holy Spirit's purpose in having me saturate myself with that particular scripture, came during a home fellowship meeting. I was singled out by one person and orally assaulted with a barrage of accusations. Although I was initially shocked, the Holy Spirit instructed me to remain calm and let her have her say. This confrontation was the enactment of what I had been meditating upon all day. Through the flesh, demon powers had attached themselves to my "hand of ministry", but these powers were to be judged.

When she had finished her hostilities, I confidently stood and shared with the group the account of Paul's shipwreck. Then, I vigorously shook my right hand, symbolically casting the viper into the fire of judgment. Thus, I broke the curse of the words, and they never had an emotional effect on me. My spirit remained clear and free, and the next morning I was able to receive the deep revelation of the demon forces of schizophrenia that had attacked me the night before.[9]

When One Speaks Evil Upon Himself

Proverbs 6:2, "Thou art snared by the words of thy mouth." The Hebrew word *yaqosh*, translated "snared", means to bring to ruin or destruction similar to a a bird being caught in a net.

---

[9] The Schizophrenia Revelation is found in our book, <u>Pigs InThe Parlor,</u> Impact Books, Inc., Kirkwood, MO. 1973, p.123.

Rebecca, Isaac's wife, was snared by the words of her mouth. She had plotted with her son, Jacob, to deceive Isaac and thereby rob his brother, Esau, of his father's blessing. Jacob feared that the deception would be discovered and he would be cursed rather than blessed. Whereupon, Rebecca declared, "Upon me be thy curse" Gen. 27:13. Behold, the curse came upon her: she never saw her son again, for she died prematurely.

Another powerful example from scripture of a spoken curse is a curse upon the entire Jewish race.

Jesus had been brought for trial before Pilate. The Jews, incited by their chief priests and elders, were demanding that Jesus be crucified.

> When Pilate saw that he could prevail nothing, but that rather a tumult was made, he took water, and washed his hands before the multitude, saying, I am innocent of the blood of this just person; see ye to it. Then answered all the people, and said, HIS BLOOD BE ON US AND ON OUR CHILDREN.
>
> Matt. 27:24,25 (Emphasis ours)

There has never been a more persecuted people on this earth than the Jews. Anti-Semitism is fiercely demonic. Six million Jews died in Hitler's death camps during World War II. In our travels we have visited two of those notorious death camps, Achawitz and Dacaau. As we stood in the chambers where thousands upon thousands were exterminated with cyanide gas, and as we gazed upon the ovens where their bodies were incinerated, we shuddered in astonishment that an atrocity of this magnitude could ever happen. The

44

indignities and cruelties imposed upon those Jews is beyond comprehension, but the curse had been spoken when Jesus stood before Pilate. The Jews declared: "HIS BLOOD BE ON US AND ON OUR CHILDREN." The curse goes on!

Many of God's people are wandering about in their own personal wilderness. Their lives are going nowhere. They are like the children of Israel in the Wilderness of Sin, making circles around Mt. Sinai. Murmuring and complaining against God -- against His appointed leaders, against where He has placed us, against what He has provided for us -- will put any one under a wilderness curse just as it did the Israelites. God said,

> How long shall I bear with this evil congregation, which murmur against me? I have heard the murmurings of the children of Israel, which they murmur against me. Say unto them, as truly as I live, saith the LORD, as ye have spoken in mine ears, so will I do to you.
> Numbers 14:27, 28

Forty years they wandered, never setting a foot in the verdant land of Canaan. The carcasses of everyone from twenty years old and upward fell in the wilderness Why did this happen? When confronted with the challenge of warfare, which was God's plan to bring them into their inheritance,

> All the children of Israel murmured against Moses and against Aaron: and the whole congregation said unto them, Would God that we had died in the land of Egypt! or WOULD

GOD WE HAD DIED IN THIS
WILDERNESS.

Numbers 14:2 (Emphasis ours)

They spoke a curse upon themselves. They were snared
by their complaining hearts and murmuring words.

Through them God warns us:

> Neither murmur ye, as some of them also
> murmured, and were destroyed of the destroyer.
> Now all these things happened unto them for
> ensamples [types] and they are written for our
> admonition, upon whom the ends of the world
> are come.
>
> I Cor. 10:10,11

OATHS

What about oaths or pledges that are taken when people
join lodges, fraternities or sororities? Jesus admonished,
"Swear not at all" Matt. 5:34. The *Amplified Bible* translates
this phrase: "Do not bind yourselves by an oath at all."
Besides, many elements in the oaths of human organizations
are ungodly. James further wrote:

> But above all things, my brethren, swear not,
> neither by heaven, neither by the earth, neither
> by ANY OTHER OATH; but let your yea be
> yea, and your nay, be nay; LEST YE FALL
> INTO CONDEMNATION.
>
> ....James 5:12, (Emphasis ours)

Freemasonry

The Masonic lodge requires all who join to take an oath. The initiate must swear under threat of death not to divulge the secrets of the lodge, saying that...

> Without the least equivocation, mental reservation, or self evasion of mind in me whatever, binding myself under no less a penalty than that of having my throat cut across, my tongue torn out by the roots and my body buried in the rough sands of the sea at low water mark, where the tide ebbs and flows every twenty-four hours. So help me God, and keep me steadfast in the due performance of the same.

In order to be delivered from the curses of Freemasonry, it is our experience that one must not only confess that he has sinned in taking the oath, but he must also destroy all paraphernalia pertaining to the lodge -- such as rings, aprons, books. If one retains any such objects, demons of curse have a legal right to that person's life.

Freemasonry, in all its branches, is basically evil. It is a bloodless religion. Although there is some emphasis upon scripture, the blood of Christ is omitted. Therefore, it is an abomination to God and brings its adherents under a curse.

Fraternities And Sororities

Fraternities and sororities are organizations usually associated with colleges and universities. They are organized around certain oaths, or pledges, and are usually secret concerning their initiation and ritual. "Most social fraternities began in semi-secrecy, possibly in imitation of

FREEMASONRY"[10]

Several people have shared with us their involvements in fraternities and sororities. They testify of their need to be delivered from curses of idolatry, control, fear, rejection and soul-ties.

One ex-fraternity man compared his being "made into a fraternity man" to a counterfeit new birth experience. His initiation involved the shedding of blood. The "first person on line" (leader) committed bestiality with a chicken, then the chicken was sacrificed.

This initiate was beaten continuously for fifteen hours, which was referred to as "crossing the burning sand." Then he was required to kneel before the Greek letters of the fraternity and repeat the fraternity pledge.

He stated, "New fraternity members became slaves to the leaders, being required to get them alcohol, drugs and girls. There were tons of fornication. I can't bring out how bad it really was."[11]

Certainly, not all fraternities are as perverted as the one our friend has described, but some of them are. "Social fraternities and sororities have been opposed as being snobbish, discriminatory, and unwise in their initiation policies."[12]

Oaths are forbidden by the Word of God, and the oaths required by fraternities and sororities bind their members in soul-ties to ungodly people and in allegience to other gods. A former sorority sister wrote to us the following testimony:

---

[10]   Academic American Encyclopedia. (1989). Grolier, Inc., Danbury, CT. Vol. 8, p. 288.
[11]   Personal testimony. Chicago, IL.
[12]   Colliers Encyclopedia, (1984). P.F. Collier, Inc., New York. Vol. 10, p.336.

I made an oath to the sorority organization by swearing on the Holy Bible. I made a covenant with the sorority, and I formed an ungodly soul-tie with the organization wherein my soul (mind, emotions and will) was committed to the sorority. I was not aware of the idolatry when I made the commitment. I had made a verbal and written vow to another god. II Corinthians 6:16 states: "And what agreement hath the temple of God with idols? for ye are the temple of the living God; as God hath said, I will dwell in them, and walk in them; and I will be their God and they shall be my people."

Paul said in II Corinthians 6:14, "Be ye not unequally yoked together with unbelievers: for what fellowship hath righteousness with unrighteousness? and what communion hath light with darkness?' I was yoked with the sorority through my oath and vow...I had made friends with the world and other gods. Friendship with the world is enmity against God (James 4:4).

I thank God, that once my eyes were open to the truth; the truth made me free. I repented to God and asked God for forgiveness for putting other gods before Him. I denounced all involvement with the sorority. I separated myself from that organization. II Corinthians 6:17, 'Wherefore come out from among them, and be ye separate, saith the Lord, and touch not the unclean thing; and I will receive you.' I destroyed all paraphernalia, rituals and artifacts. I received deliverance from ungodly soul-ties, idolatry and rejection. I was purged and cleansed from the sin of idolatry. The curses were broken from over my life, and the Lord has caused me to walk, not under the curse, but in freedom through the blood of Jesus.[13]

The Hippocratic Oath

The Hippocratic Oath, still used in the graduation ceremonies of many medical schools and displayed on the office walls of many physicians, is an ethical code attributed to the ancient Greek physician, Hippocrates. Hippocrates is traditionally regarded as "the father of medicine". The ethical standards contained in the oath are commendable; however, it IS an oath, and Jesus said, "Do not bind yourself by an oath at all" Matt. 5:34, Ampified Bible.

Furthermore, the oath is based upon out-and-out idolatry, when it swears to certain Greek gods. The following is the introduction to the Hippocratic Oath. Judge for yourself:

> I swear by Apollo the physician and Aesculapius and health and all-heal and all the gods and goddesses, that according to my ability and judgment I will keep this oath and this stipulation.

Apollo is from the Greek word *apollynai* meaning "destroy"; the same root word for Apollyon (Rev. 9:11) referring to the devil or Satan, the angel of the bottomless pit. In Greek and Roman mythology, Apollo is the god of archery, prophecy, medicine, poetry and music. He was always represented as being the highest type of masculine beauty and grace; later identified with Helios, a sun god.

---

[13]   Personal testimony. Chicago, IL

Aesculapius is, in mythology, the god of medicine, the son of Apollo by nymph Coronis.

What does God's word say about swearing to other gods?

> And in all things that I have said unto you be circumspect: and MAKE NO MENTION OF THE NAME OF OTHER GODS, NEITHER LET IT BE HEARD OUT OF THY MOUTH.
>
> Exod. 23:13 (Emphasis ours)

> That ye come not among these nations, these that remain among you; NEITHER MAKE MENTION OF THE NAME OF THEIR GODS, NOR CAUSE TO SWEAR BY THEM, neither serve them, nor bow yourselves unto them.
>
> Josh. 23:7 (Emphasis ours)

A young medical doctor shared with us about his medical school's graduating class being required to take the Hippocratic Oath. He was thankful that it was done in a group ceremony where everyone repeated the vow together. It gave him the opportunity to interject the name of Jesus while others were saying the names of Apollo and Aesculapius.

Doctors who have taken the Hippocratic Oath, and who are now walking in the light, should repent of the sin of vowing to false gods, beseech God's forgiveness, renounce these gods of Greece and Rome, destroy any copies of the oath in their possession and receive deliverance from demons of curse.

51

6

AUTHORITY ENGENDERED CURSES

Over and over again in Paul's letters to the churches we find him saying, "Grace to you and peace from God". Paul was a spiritual father over those to whom he wrote, and he blessed them with these words of grace and peace. As one with delegated authority from God, Paul had the power to bless, and he wisely and consistently exercised this authority.

Inherent in the authority to bless is the authority to curse: the two cannot be separated, anymore than the two sides of a coin can be separated. It is an awesome responsibility to possess delegated authority from God. The same authority that makes a blessing effective also makes a curse effective. Therefore, all in authority "will be judged more strictly" Jas. 3:1,NIV.

All authority is vested in God, and God has chosen to exercise His rule through the delegation of authority to men and angels. The Word of God declares that, "there is no authority except that which God has established" Rom. 13:1, NIV. Delegated authorities include kings and all civil magistrates, husbands, parents and church leaders.

Not only does an authority bless or curse, with words, those who are submitted to him, but he blesses or curses them through his righteousness or the lack thereof.

> When the righteous are in authority the people
> rejoice: but when the wicked beareth rule, the
> people mourn.   Prov. 29:2

In reading through the succession of kings who ruled over Israel and Judah, we find that some walked in the ways of the Lord, and others were evil. The nations fared according to the spiritual condition of their rulers.

Jehosaphat, for example, "set himself to seek the Lord...so the realm of Jehosaphat was quiet: for his God gave him rest round about" II Chron. 20:3,30. His son, Jehoram, then came to the throne of Judah. Jehoram had married the daughter of the wicked King Ahab, and "wrought that which was evil in the eyes of the Lord" II Chron. 21:6. He murdered his brothers to protect his throne and set up places of idol worship. Therefore, elements of his kingdom revolted against him, and a great plague from the Lord smote the people. God cursed Jehoram with an incurable disease of the bowels, and Jehoram died in great pain.

Ahaziah then became king. His mother, the wicked Athaliah, was his counselor. The nation was in turmoil until Ahaziah was killed by Jehu, God's appointed man to execute judgment. Athaliah, was also slain, "And all **the people of the land rejoiced; and the city was quiet,** after that they had slain Athaliah with the sword" I Chron. 23:21 (Emphasis ours).

When a ruler is guided by Divine wisdom, he will be a blessing; when he forsakes God's counsel he will be a curse, for His judgments and influence will be unjust and perverse.

In the book of Proverbs, "wisdom" is personified. Wisdom is Christ. In the New Testament, Paul speaks of

Christ, "In whom are hid all the treasures of wisdom and knowledge" Col. 2:3. Wisdom asserts,

> Counsel and sound judgment are mine; I have understanding and power. By me kings reign and rulers make laws that are just.
>
> Prov. 8:14,15, NIV

Unwise rulers open spiritual doors through which wicked spirits can attack those under their authority. Thus, a husband who is neglectful and insensitive to his wife's need for godly headship makes her vulnerable to insecurity with its many fears. A minister who utilizes control tactics to dominate his congregation exposes the people to powers of witchcraft. A head of government whose lifestyle is immoral or whose policies are anti-biblical jeopardizes the entire nation. This is how those in authority sometimes bring families, churches and nations under a curse.

Believers are exhorted to pray for all in authority in order to enjoy God's blessings.

> I urge, then, first of all, that requests, prayers, intercession and thanksgiving be made for everyone -- for kings and all those in authority, that we may live peaceful and quiet lives in all godliness and holiness.
>
> I Tim. 2:1,2, NIV

Thus, we are instructed to pray for the president of our nation, his cabinet, all congressmen and judges of the land. Whether they make decisions and uphold legislation based upon the principles of God's Word, will determine how God deals with the nation: whether it is blessed or cursed.

What shall we ask God to do when an authority over us walks in disobedience to God's commandments? For one thing, we should ask God to send a prophet to confront that leader. Throughout scripture we find God sending His prophets to warn the wicked. Let us look at a few examples.

When King Jehoram set up places of idol worship and "caused the inhabitants of Jerusalem to commit fornication" II Chron. 21:11, Elijah, the prophet, wrote the king a letter saying that because Jehoram had not walked in the righteous ways of his father, "Behold, with a great plague will the Lord smite thy people, and thy children, and thy wives, and all thy goods" II Chron. 21:14.

When the princes of Judah left the house of the Lord God and served idols, God "sent prophets to them, to bring them again unto the Lord" II Chron. 24:19. The princes did not heed the prophets; therefore, God sent the host of Syria against them, and the Syrians executed the judgment that God had decreed (See: II Chron. 24:17-25).

When King Amaziah slaughtered the Edomites, he brought back their gods and made them to be his gods. The anger of the Lord was kindled against Amaziah, and "he sent unto him a prophet" who challenged the foolishness of the king. (See: II Chron. 25:14,15, 27).

Remember, also, that God sent the prophet Samuel to confront rebellious King Saul (See: I Sam. 15:22,23), and He sent John the Baptist to rebuke King Herod for "all the evils which Herod had done" and especially for taking the wife of his brother, Philip (See: Matt. 14:3-5; Lk. 3:19,20).

Therefore, whenever we find ourselves in a situation where an authority over us is walking contrary to the ways of God, we should pray God to send a prophet to speak into that situation. That ruler will either repent or God will remove him.

Founding Father Curses

The founding of organizations is a crucial aspect of authority engendered curses. Authority figures sometimes bring organizations into being. Therefore, we must be wise to inquire, "What is at the foundation of an organization? What was in the life of the founding father? Was something amiss or askew when that foundation was laid?"

Everything built upon a foundation is affected by the foundation itself. The principle of curses being passed down from founding fathers is as old as the human race. Adam was the first man. The human race was founded upon Adam.

> Wherefore, as by one man sin entered into the world, and death by sin; and so death passed upon all men, for that all have sinned...by this one man's offence death reigned by one.
>
> Rom. 5:12,17

In the same way that curses pass down through the generations of a family, curses pass down through the generations of a business, profession, government, local church or any kind of organization. If sin curses are found in the founding fathers, the curses will pass down through succeeding generations. Therefore, it is vital to examine the roots of whatever organization with which we become identified.

Some churches get started in wrong ways by the wrong people. Over the years, we have watched the up and down cycles of a church formed out of a church split. Those who organized the new church were determined to run the church and its pastor. Every time the church had begun to progress there had been a conflict between the pastor (they have had a succession of pastors) and those who oppose authority. This church is cursed.

What we are saying about curses passing down from founding fathers is illustrated by the chiropractic profession. There are Christian chiropractors who love the Lord and who would be appalled at the suggestion that they are in any way associated with the occult. Yet, the founder of chiropractic, DD. Palmer, was deeply involved in the occult. In his own written testimony he states that he was a magnetic healer for nine years before he discovered the principles that comprise the methods known as chiropractic.

Through magnetic healing and chiropractic techniques, Palmer was attempting to adjust the "innate power", or existing life flow, within the body. This is what the ancient Chinese called "Ch'i" (pronounced "key".) Chinese medicine teaches that illness occurs when the flow of the Ch'i is either excessive, restricted or blocked in a particular area of the body, thus disrupting the balance of yin and yang. It is claimed that healing occurs when the flow of the Ch'i is regulated, and the proper balance between yin and yang is restored. Various techniques have been employed by occultists to regulate the Ch'i: acupuncture (needles inserted in strategic parts of the body), acupressure (substituting finger pressure for needles), myotherapy (manipulating "trigger points" in the body), orgonomy (sexual orgasm), reflexology (pressure points on hands and feet), rolfing (intense massage), magnet power (magnets passed over the body) and herbal applications.

The following quotation is from Chapter 11 of Palmer's textbook on chiropractic, (still used in chiropractic colleges today), "The Inner Power Speaks":

> We chiropractors work with the subtle substance of the soul. We release the prisoned impulse, the tiny rivulet of force that emanates from the mind and flows over the nerves to the cells and stirs them to life. We deal with the magic power that transforms common food into living, loving, thinking clay; that robes the earth with beauty, and hues and scents the flowers with the glory of the air. In the dim, dark, distant long ago, when the sun first bowed to the morning star, this power spoke and there was life; it quickened the slime of the sea and the dust of the earth and drove the cell to union with its fellow in countless living forms. Through eons of time, it finned the fish and winged the bird and fanged the beast. Endlessly it worked, evolving its forms until it produced the crowning glory of them all. With tireless energy it blows the bubble of each individual life and then silently, relentlessly dissolves the form, and absorbs the spirit into itself again. And you ask, can chiropractic cure appendicitis or the flu? Have you more faith in a knife or a spoonful of medicine than the innate power that animates the internal living world?

DD. Palmer was an avowed occult practitioner, a pantheist and an evolutionist, to say the least. This evil is at the root of the chiropractic practice that he fostered. Several Christian chiropractors whom we have consulted, tell us that they do not manipulate the life force, and do not follow Palmer's teachings in this regard. Wonderful! Yet, we believe it is necessary for Christian chiropractors to renounce all association with DD. Palmer's occult practices and false doctrines. Then, they can break all curses that have passed down to them through DD. Palmer and be delivered of the demons of such curses.

We have found no problems with the physical therapy aspects of chiropractic. We agree with a chiropractor who wrote, "Research done by scientists and medical doctors proves that manual manipulation is an effective and sometimes preferred alternative to drug therapy."

Still, it deeply concerns us that more and more chiropractors are taking up such New Age occult practices as acupuncture, acupressure and reflexology. It is understandable that chiropractors would so readily adopt New Age occult techniques, for these methods are allied with those explored by the founder of chiropractic. Both practitioners and their clients come under a curse when occult techniques are employed.

Frank relates his own experience with a chiropractor in 1977:

A back strain led to an acute attack of sciatica, a very painful condition in the hip and thigh. For a month I had been unable to sit or lie down without excruciating pain. I decided to go to a chiropractor for physical therapy to relieve the pressure on the sciatic nerve.

The doctor's diagnostic procedure included running a metal probe around the surface of one ear. I didn't think much about this until he repeated the procedure on my next two visits. I observed that the probe was attached to a small wire that was connected to a little, black box. Occasionally, the box emitted a slight electronic beep.

I finally inquired, "What are you doing to my ear? What does that have to do with my treatment for sciatica? He replied, "Oh, let me show you what I'm doing." He unrolled a large chart with an ear drawn on it. The picture of a human embryo was superimposed over that of the ear. The doctor explained, "The ancient Chinese discovered thousands of years ago that the ear is in the shape of an embryo. By placing the form of an embryo over a picture of an ear we know that certain points on the ear correspond to certain points of the body. I am treating your sciatica by putting a very slight electrical charge into your ear at the point that corresponds to your hip and leg. This instrument is also diagnostic. I have determined that you also have a problem in your kidneys, and I am treating that, too."

As soon as I returned home I called the other pastor in our church. I said, "Jimmy, I need deliverance." Jimmy wanted to know why I thought that I needed deliverance. I said, "I have been involved in the occult. I have just had electrical acupuncture." I was serious!

We are discovering too many of God's people who are inadvertently becoming exposed to New Age occult practices through chiropractic and other unsuspected sources. Some medical nurses today are trained in "touch therapy" as an avenue of healing power. Beauticians and manicurists are being taught acupressure in their colleges. It has been added to their textbooks. We know of the owner of a health food store who asks permission to look into the eyes of her customers. She practices iridology, a form of divination, to diagnose current and future health problems.

We are not labeling all chiropractors, nurses, and beauticians as occult practitioners. However, we are saying loud and clear that New Age occult practices are invading many professions, social services and businesses. We are being exposed to more and more New Age occult practices in the least suspected places. We must heed God's Word:

> See then that ye walk circumspectly, not as fools, but as wise, redeeming the time, because the days are evil.
>
> Eph. 5:15,16

7

WITCHCRAFT CURSES

There are two spiritual power sources: God and Satan. Servants of The Most High God use their delegated spiritual authority to bless others and to defeat the devil. Emissaries of Satan employ Satan's power to curse, control and harm. This evil, supernatural power over people and their affairs is known as witchcraft or sorcery.

God's Word absolutely condemns and forbids all witchcraft practices.

> Let no one be found among you who sacrifices his son or daughter in the fire, who practices divination or sorcery, interprets omens, engages in witchcraft, or casts spells, or who is a medium or spiritist or who consults the dead. Anyone who does these things is detestable to the Lord.
>
> Deut. 18:10-12, NIV

Witches or wizards were condemned to death under the Law of Moses (See: Lev. 20:27). God's word is emphatic in condemning all that today is called "the black arts".

Control of others is witchcraft's appeal. The witch and wizard, and those who seek after them, attempt to control others, endeavoring to gain some advantage over their fellow men.   The power is real, but it is the devil's power, and its end is ruin.

The history of Israel records times when God's people ignored God and turned to the powers of darkness for help. They thought that the sorcerers would solve their crises. God rebuked and judged Israel for relying upon witchcraft:

> When men tell you to consult mediums and spiritists, who whisper and mutter, should not a people inquire of their God? Why consult the dead on behalf of the living? To the law and to the testimony! If they do not speak according to this word, they have no light of dawn. Distressed and hungry, they will roam through the land; when they are famished, they will become enraged and, looking upward, will curse their king and their God.
>
> Isaiah :19-21, NIV

The influence of witchcraft has increased in our own nation and society in recent years. "The whole world lies in wickedness" I John 5:19, for "the great dragon...that old serpent, called the Devil, and Satan...deceiveth the whole world" Rev. 12:9. God said that the devil would deceive the whole world, and we are seeing it fulfilled.

The devil's deceptions are also infiltrating the Body of Christ. Witchcraft is spreading into many local fellowships through New Age influences. Many Christians are turning to powers other than God in quest of healing, guidance and power.

We were invited to minister in church in a small Texas city. Before the service began, we noticed eight or ten people lined up in front of a man who seemed to be laying hands on them for healing. To our dismay we learned that the man was dealing in Myotherapy, a form of acupressure. He was pressing the palms of people's hands to heal them. This was routinely taking place in the aisle of a charismatic fellowship. The leadership of the church had questioned the practice and was relieved when we brought it into the light of God's Word.

Our burden for the Church today is expressed by Paul's concern over the church at Corinth:

> I am afraid that just as Eve was deceived by the
> serpent's cunning, your minds may somehow be
> led astray from your sincere and pure devotion
> to Christ.
>
> II Cor. 11:3, NIV

Witches employ incantations, potions, herbal concoctions and other magical arts to bring about curses. There are many plausible accounts of people who have suffered and even died due to witchcraft curses sent against them.

A couple who were classmates of ours in seminary went to Africa as missionaries. Their first letter to us from Africa related their awe over the power of witch doctors to afflict people with curses. They had seen people die from such curses. Their seminary training had not prepared them to confront these evil spiritual powers.

Most Christians today would consider it unbelievable that witchcraft would have such power. Ezekiel prophesied to women who were doing some kind of witchcraft or voodoo.

Woe to the women who sew magic charms on all their wrists and make veils of various lengths for their heads in order to ensnare people...By lying to my people, who listen to lies, you have killed those who should not have died and have spared those who should not live.

Ezek. 13:18,19, NIV

Maria needed deliverance. A couple in our church brought her to us. She was a very nervous, fearful and distraught individual who was tormented by severe headaches.

Maria was from Venezuela, South America. She had met and married a man from the United States. He was employed by an American oil company doing work in Venezuela.

In a pre-deliverance counseling session we learned that Maria was a young believer in Christ whose family in Venezuela was deeply involved in witchcraft. She, her sister and her mother had held hands, standing in a circle, and made a pact that they would never be separated. When Maria accompanied her husband to the States, her mother and sister put curses on her for breaking her vow. Maria explained that her mother kept a live owl, bat and tarantula spider as instruments for putting curses on people.

When we commanded the demons to leave Maria, a spirit of death manifested by cutting off her breath, and her face contorted grotesquely as the demons were cast out. Deliverance from witchcraft spirits is often accompanied by strong manifestations.

We were thankful that Maria started coming to our fellowship meetings to receive teachings that would help her to maintain her deliverance. She was a changed person. The powers of witchcraft had been defeated.

James, a young soldier, was another person delivered from witchcraft curses. We met him at a deliverance conference we were conducting in California.

James was a native of Jamaica. His father, uncle and he were deeply involved in voodoo. Then, James became a Christian, and, being uncomfortable with his family's heavy occult activities, moved to the United States to get away from that influence. We found James to be very tormented and oppressed. An evil spirit came upon him every night and attacked him sexually. We explained that this spirit is called "succubus"; a female demon that comes at night to sleeping males and gives them the sensation of having sexual relations.[14]

A feeling of uncleanness overwhelmed James. He had tried everything he knew to get release from this tormenting spirit, but to no avail. In his ignorance of the demonic supernatural realm, he had consulted a witch in New England where he was then stationed in the army.

The witch instructed him to go home and get an egg. He was to bring the egg in his hand, traveling quite a distance on a bus. The egg must not be broken. The witch performed a ritual over the egg. She then instructed James to place the egg on the floor and crush it with his foot. If a serpent came out of the egg it would be a sign that he was set free from the succubus.

---

[14]   The female counterpart to *succubus* is *incubus*, an unclean spirit that comes at night to lie on sleeping women to have sexual intercourse with them.

James did as he was instructed, and, when he crushed the egg, out came a serpent! However, he soon discovered that the succubus was stronger than ever. His going to the occult for help only compounded his problem. Satan does not "cast out Satan" Matt. 12:26.

We led James in a prayer of confession and renunciation of the sins of witchcraft. In the mighty name of Jesus we cast out the spirit of succubus and many other evil spirits. "If the Son therefore shall make you free, ye shall be free indeed" John 8:36.

We took time to teach James how to use his own spiritual authority as a believer in Jesus Christ. He then knew that should any of the spirits try to return he could drive them away in the name of Jesus.

We began to learn first-hand about witchcraft curses while pastoring in a city with a strong Mexican-American culture that is steeped in witchcraft. We were reaching people for Christ out of this culture, and most of them had major problems from witchcraft curses.

A ringing phone jarred us out of a deep sleep. A glance at the clock told us that it was 2:00 a.m. It was Rita, a young woman who had attended a few services at our church. She was very excited and very urgent. She wanted Frank to come to her house as quickly as possibly.

When I arrived at Rita's home, I found her brother, Alberto, a husky farm laborer, lying on the couch. He was too weak to move. He seemed at the point of death. Rita had seen us cast demons out of people, and she had tried to cast demons out of her brother. She showed me marks on her legs where the demons had attacked her and bit her. She was hysterical.

I began to pray for Alberto. I commanded the spirits of witchcraft to release him. In a few minutes he sat up and asked for food. He had not eaten since getting home from the farm.

I was reminded of the sons of Sceva who attempted to cast demons out of a demonized man "by Jesus whom Paul preacheth...And the man in whom the evil spirit was leaped on them and overcame them" Acts 19:13,16. The sons of Sceva were not believers in Christ and, therefore, had no spiritual authority over demons.

This was Rita's problem. She was attempting to cast out demons in the name of the Jesus that Brother Frank talked about. She did not yet have a personal relationship with Christ. Soon afterward she gave her heart to the Lord and was soon helping to minister deliverance to others.

Lupe was a new convert in our congregation. She lived with her mother and elderly grandmother. Lupe confided in us that her grandmother was a witch. She used stuffed animals and other paraphernalia to work her witchcraft.

When the grandmother died, Lupe asked her two pastors, Brother Hammond and Brother Low, to pray over their house. She and her mother were experiencing some strange things. Three or four hours after sweeping and dusting the house it would be dirty again. When one of them would sit in grandmother's chair, something would prick their legs. They had examined the chair and found there was no natural cause for the pricking. Furthermore, there had been several apparitions of grandmother since her death.

We two pastors went through the house room by room. Every item that had belonged to the grandmother that might have been used for witchcraft was destroyed. We anointed the walls with oil and commanded every spirit of witchcraft to get out. No closet or cabinet was overlooked. The cleansing of the house was effective. None of the problems reoccurred.

There is a biblical account of attempted witchcraft from which we learn several valuable truths. It is the account in Numbers, chapters twenty-two through twenty-four, of King Balak hiring Balaam to curse the Israelites. Balaam was a prominent sorcerer in the region who, because of his ability to effect curses, was considered worthy of substantial payment for his services.

The Israelites had come up out of Egypt, had defeated the Amorite kings and were now camped on the borders of Moab. Balak the Moabite king was afraid. The only chance he could see of defeating the Israelites was for them to be cursed by Balaam. Witchcraft was a recognized way of getting an advantage over others.

Balaam had a solid reputation of being able to curse people. His ability to impose curses on others was no mere superstition. King Balak testified: "I know that those you bless are blessed, and those you curse are cursed" Num. 22:6. Yes, witchcraft curses are real!

In spite of Balaam's lust for reward he could only speak blessings upon God's people. God sovereignly intervened and prevented Israel from being cursed. Moses testified:

> The Lord thy God would not hearken unto Balaam; but the Lord thy God turned the curse into a blessing unto thee, because the Lord thy God loved thee.
>
> Deut. 23:5

Why was Balaam unable to curse Israel? All unbelief and rebellion had been purged out of their midst. When the cloud moved, they moved. They were God's people, walking in obedience to Him. Therefore, they were blessed of God.

Balak became impatient and angry toward Balaam. Why had he not cursed Israel? Balaam announced:

> How shall I curse, whom God hath not cursed? or how shall I defy, whom the Lord hath not defied?
>
> Num. 23:8

What do we learn from Balaam's inability to curse Israel? When we are walking in obedience before God, the curse cannot alight. All who qualify for God's blessings are immune from witchcraft curses.

We must not become paranoid, fearing that someone is putting curses on us. Our protection from witchcraft is simply living in righteousness and holiness before God.

Too, we must remain vigilant, for the devil is always roaming about as a roaring lion seeking whom he may devour.

In Numbers, chapter twenty-five, we discover that the Israelites committed whoredom with the daughters of Moab. They also "bowed down to their gods" Num. 25:2.

The judgment of God fell upon Israel and 24,000 perished! Who was the devil's instrument? Balaam!

> Behold, these (the leaders of the people) caused the children of Israel, **through the counsel of Balaam,** to commit trespass against the Lord in the matter of Peor, and there was a plague

among the congregation of the Lord.

Num. 31:16 (Emphasis ours)

Thank God, Christians today are learning their authority in God. They are becoming wise in knowing how to protect themselves from witchcraft and how to cancel the powers of witchcraft.

How can a Christian protect himself from witchcraft curses? Our protection is in putting on the whole armor of God. It is all the protection required. As Christian soldiers we must keep on the girdle of truth, the breastplate of righteousness, the helmet of salvation and the shield of faith. Our feet must be shod with a readiness to proclaim the gospel of peace and wield the sword of the Spirit which is the Word of God. (Eph. 6:13-17). The whole armor of God is our defense.

A brave soldier of the Cross is not awed by the devil. He knows his weapons and his authority. We must never tremble at the powers of witchcraft nor cringe at the threats they pose, but remain strong in the Lord and the power of His might. Jesus promised:

> Behold, I give unto you power to tread on serpents and scorpions, and over all the power of the enemy: and nothing shall by any means hurt you.

Luke 10:19

For any who know, or think, that they have been exposed to witchcraft curses, we urge the prayers and confessions in Chapter 9.

8

LAWS GOVERNING CURSES

There are eight basic laws that govern curses. These laws apply to each category of curses: generation curses, personal sin curses, accursed things, word curses, founding father curses and witchcraft curses.

1. THERE IS A CAUSE FOR EVERY CURSE.

> Like a fluttering sparrow or a darting swallow,
> an undeserved curse does not come to rest.
> Prov. 26:2, NIV

A person cannot inadvertently stumble into a curse. Curses are regulated by spiritual law: God's law. In fact, it is God who decides whether one is cursed or blessed, and His decision is based upon one's obedience to His commandments.

> If thou wilt not hearken unto the voice of the Lord thy God, to observe to do all his commandments and his statutes...all these curses shall come upon thee, and overtake thee.
> Deut. 28:15

Blessings as well as curses are subject to Divine regulation. One does not stumble into the blessings of God.

> If thou shalt hearken diligently unto the voice of the Lord thy God, to observe and to do all his commandments...all these blessing shall come upon thee.
>
> Deut. 28:1,2

2. SIN IS THE GATEWAY FOR THE CURSE

The first curses upon the human race came in the Garden of Eden when Adam and Eve sinned. Everyone involved in the sin was cursed.

The serpent was cursed:
> So, the LORD God said to the serpent, BECAUSE YOU HAVE DONE THIS, CURSED ARE YOU.
>
> Gen. 3:14

The woman was cursed:
> I will greatly increase your pains in child-bearing; with pain you will give birth to children. Your desire will be for your husband, and he will rule over you.
>
> Gen. 3:16, NIV

Adam was cursed:
> Because you listened to your wife and ate from the tree about which I commanded you, You must not eat of it, CURSED IS THE GROUND BECAUSE OF YOU; through painful toil you will eat of it all the days of your life.
>
> Gen. 3:17, NIV (Emphasis ours)

Remember, "A curse causeless shall not come" Prov. 26:2. The curses came in Eden, and the cause was sin. Therefore, sin is the root cause for the curse. As long as the root remains, the curse cannot be broken.

Nowadays, too few people attribute problems in life to curses. For example, when a farmer gets into problems with his crops, does he look for a sin cause in his own life? No, he will no doubt use every possible means to try to remedy his endangered crops. He will resort to fertilizers, herbicides, insecticides, irrigation water and whatever else he can find. However, according to the Word of God, agricultural hardships are due to curses. (See: Deut. 27:23,24).

We cannot reverse spiritual problems with fleshly weapons. A curse is a spiritual problem that requires a spiritual solution.

Many physical afflictions and many financial plights are due to curses. Frank shares this testimony:

From the age of ten I began to suffer severely from allergies. Asthma was so severe that it was common for me to miss as many as thirty days out of a school term. I would lie in bed for a week or two at a time, struggling for every breath. There was little medical relief to be had. My parents resorted to every remedy offered by anyone, much of which was pure superstition..

Someone told my mother that it would cure my asthma if I would smoke dried fig leaves in a corncob pipe. All this treatment did was blister my tongue. There was another remedy we tried. My height was marked on the wall of a closet. A hole was bored in the wall at my height. A lock of my hair was placed in the hole. It was believed that when I grew past the hole containing the lock of hair that I would be cured. These superstitious practices only compounded my infirmities.

Hay fever also plagued me. It was especially severe in the fall of the year when ragweed and other pollens filled the air. The hay fever was so severe that I was unable to function for days at a time. When the Lord called me to a travel ministry, I told the Lord that I could not travel in September and October because pollens caused severe hay fever.

When I reached my late 40's, I began to learn about curses: their causes and effects. Our house had its share of idolatrous pictures and figurines. In addition, the walls and shelves were full of American Indian artifacts, including a number of idolatrous objects. The Lord reminded me that I had started collecting Indian artifacts at age ten, the same year that my allergies started.

We had a thorough house cleaning. Everything suspect was broken, burned or disposed of in some way. With the help of others in the fellowship, I went through a thorough deliverance. The demons of curse were cast out, and the suffering ended!

3. A CURSE IS A SPIRITUAL PROBLEM WHICH CANNOT BE REMEDIED BY NATURAL MEANS.

> Be not deceived; God is not mocked: for whatsoever a man soweth, that shall he also reap.
>
> Gal. 6:7

Hosea prophesied God's coming judgment upon Israel because of her idolatry. They had sown to the wind and would reap the whirlwind (Hos. 8:7). Even though Israel paid tribute to Assyria, that would not buy her security, for Israel remained under a curse because of her calf-worship. Likewise, anyone under a curse cannot escape through human ingenuity.

When sickness and disease are due to a curse, no science of man will extricate a person. When the tithe is withheld; there will be a curse upon one's resources, and no amount of planning and toil will curb the devourer.

Oh, but we can think of people who have robbed God in tithes and offering and they still have wealth. Yes, but as God said through Malachi, "I will even send a curse upon you, and I will curse your blessings" Mal. 2:2. No, God is not mocked. Even one's wealth can become a curse.

6. WHERE SIN REMAINS, THE CURSE REMAINS.

Solomon had just dedicated the beautiful temple, and the glory of the Lord filled the house. Although God dwelled in their midst, they must continue to walk in obedience; otherwise, God would send a curse:

> If I shut up heaven that there be no rain, or if I command the locusts to devour the land, or if I send pestilence among the people...

However, through repentance new blessings would come:

> IF MY PEOPLE WHICH ARE CALLED BY MY NAME, SHALL HUMBLE THEMSELVES, AND PRAY, AND SEEK MY FACE, AND TURN FROM THEIR WICKED WAYS; THEN WILL I HEAR FROM

HEAVEN, AND WILL FORGIVE THEIR SIN,
AND WILL HEAL THEIR LAND.

I Chron. 7:13,14 (Emphasis ours)

Demons have inroads where sin remains. A curse can end only when the sin behind it is confessed and forsaken and God's forgiveness obtained.

5. THE POWER OF A CURSE IS DEMONIC.

God pronounces a curse, and Satan and his demons are the instruments that carry it out. To express it another way: when a curse is imposed, God lifts His restraining hand and the devil is permitted to work.

Again, returning to Genesis 3, we find in verse fourteen the enmity that God put between the serpent and mankind through His curse upon them both. "He [the seed of woman] will crush your head, and you [Serpent] will strike his heel."

Thus, it was man's sin that gave power to that old serpent, the devil, to strike man's heel. When our wonderful Lord Jesus took our sins upon Himself, the Serpent was able to strike THE Seed of woman, but Jesus crushed his head! The cross and resurrection of Christ provided for us deliverance from the curse.

In the fourth chapter of Genesis we read about Cain and Abel, the sons of Adam and Eve. Cain became jealous and angry because God accepted Abel's blood sacrifice and rejected his own fruit sacrifice. God saw Cain's jealous anger and warned him:

Why are you angry? Why is your face downcast? If you do what is right, will you not

be accepted? But if you do not what is right,
sin is crouching at your door; it desires to have
you, but you must master it.

Gen. 4:6,7, NIV

Sin personified was crouching at Cain's door. It was
like a ferocious beast waiting for an opportunity to spring in
through the sin door into his life. Unless he repented and
obeyed God, an evil spirit would get in.

We all know what it is like for one's dog to be outside
the house wanting to get in. He will wait beside the door.
When he hears footsteps inside the house, his ears will come
to attention. When he hears a hand on the door knob, he is
poised to spring inside. It doesn't take much of an opening for
him to get in.

This is a picture of Cain's situation -- and ours. Sin
personified, a devil's emissary, waits for an opening to leap in
with his curse. All he needs is for the sin door to be opened.
This is why we are exhorted:

Do not let the sun go down while you are still
angry, and do not give the devil a foothold.

Eph. 4:26,27, NIV

If one goes to bed without repenting of his anger, he
has left the sin door open. He shouldn't be surprised in the
morning to find a pig in his parlor.

King Saul was instructed by the Lord to destroy every
Amalekite and all their livestock. Saul disobeyed God and
took King Agag alive along with the best of his cattle, sheep
and oxen. For this sin, King Saul received a curse: "an evil
spirit from the Lord troubled him" I Sam. 16:14. Saul became

paranoid; extremely jealous and suspicious of David. He pursued David and attempted time after time to kill him.

The curse of mental illness came upon King Saul because of rebellion, which is as the sin of witchcraft. Sin is the door through which a curse enters. The power behind a curse is an evil spirit.

Often, a curse is looked upon as a special category of demonization, as though a "demon of curse" is somehow different from other evil spirits. Yet, in reality, to have any evil spirit is to be cursed, and to be cursed is to have an evil spirit.

6. THE LAW PROVIDED NO REMEDY FOR A CURSE.

There was no grace imparted to those who sinned under the law. The curse came without remedy. The Word of God declares:

> For as many as are of the works of the law are under the curse; for it is written, Cursed is every one that continueth not in all things which are written in the book of the law to do them.
>
> Gal. 3:10

Since all have sinned and come short of the glory of God, and none is righteous, the curse has come upon every individual upon the face of the earth.

David's is a case in point. David violated the commandments: "Thou shall not commit adultery" and "Thou shalt not kill." Did not David repent? Indeed, he repented with bitter tears. Read Psalm 51, and refresh your memory of his pleas for God's forgiveness and favor.

Still, when Nathan confronted David, he announced the curse that God had imposed:

> Now therefore the sword shall never depart from thine house...Behold, I will raise up evil against thee out of thine own house, and I will take thy wives before thine eyes, and give them unto thy neighbour, and he shall lie with thy wives in the sight of this sun...because by this deed thou hast given great occasion to the enemies of the Lord to blaspheme...the child also that is born unto thee shall surely die.
>
> II Sam. 12:10,11,14

Even though David sincerely repented, the spoken judgment came upon him and passed down through his family. Under the law there was no remedy for a curse.

Under the law, curses from idolatry passed down to the third and fourth generations (Exod. 20:5). When a child was conceived out of wedlock, the curse passed down to the tenth generation (Deut. 23:2). Once a curse was set in motion, no recourse was provided by the law. Thank God for Jesus!

7. CHRIST REDEEMED US FROM THE CURSE OF THE LAW.

We have considered the bad news that under the law there was no remedy for a curse. Now we come to the good news: Christ has provided a way of escape.

> CHRIST HAS REDEEMED US FROM THE CURSE OF THE LAW, BEING MADE A CURSE FOR US, FOR IT IS WRITTEN,

CURSED IS EVERYONE THAT HANGETH
ON A TREE.

> Gal. 3:13 (Emphasis ours)

How did Jesus redeem us from the curse of the law? He became our Sin-Bearer: our Substitute. He took upon Himself the penalty of sin due us, and bore it in His own body on the cross.

> Who his own self bare our sins in his own body on the tree, that we being dead to sins, should live unto righteousness: by whose stripes ye were healed.
>
> I Peter 2:24

The law given through Moses imposed curses upon all who disobeyed God's commands. These curses affect the body, the mind, relationships, life's sustenance, freedom, environment, and over-all well being.

The cross is, therefore, the focus of the Gospel and rightly so. Jesus has redeemed us from the curse of the law. In practical terms this means that there is no longer any reason for any person to remain under any curse. The remedy is at hand.

8. THE REDEMPTION MUST BE APPROPRIATED.

Galatians 3:14 discloses the benefit provided through Christ's redemptive work: "That the blessing of Abraham might come on the Gentiles through Jesus Christ."

How was Abraham blessed? "The Lord blessed Abraham IN ALL THINGS" Gen. 24:1. Now, Abraham

81

obtained all of God's blessings through faith and not by obedience to the law. It is the same for us. The blessings of God must be appropriated by faith rather than by works.

It is most significant that the declaration of Abraham's blessing is connected with his willingness to sacrifice his son, Isaac: a type of God's sacrifice of His only son. God said to Abraham:

> Because thou hast done this thing, and hast not withheld thy son, thine only son: That in blessing I will bless thee...
>
> Gen. 22:17

God goes on to renew His covenant with Abraham. Indeed, it is through the new covenant, provided through the blood of Jesus, that we have our remedy from the curse imposed by the law.

Jesus died for all, but all are not saved. Why? The remedy must be appropriated. Many of God's children remain under various curses of the law. Why? They have not appropriated Christ's redemption from the curse.

Ah! We discover a common theological flaw. The full provision of the cross does not come automatically with the new birth. Otherwise, how could a Christian be sick? For, by his stripes we were healed (I Pet. 2:24). There is a God-given way to appropriate eternal life, and there are ways in which we are to appropriate healing and deliverance.

We are no longer under the law that was based upon performance-acceptance, but we are now under grace that is based upon faith. **Grace does not mean that one is immune from curses, but that there is now a remedy.**

Failure to obey God still brings a curse, but now there is a remedy. For example, God has commanded us to forgive all who trespass against us. If I refuse to forgive, I have transgressed God's commandment. The penalty is that I am turned over by God to tormenting spirits. However, I don't have to be tormented by the devil. I can repent, forgive the one who has wronged me and cast out the spirits of bitterness and torment.

Deliverance is a necessary step in being freed from curses. Since the power of a curse is demonic, the demons holding a curse in effect must be cast out. Why not just stand in faith? Because, "Faith, if it hath not works, is dead, being alone" James 2:17. Dead faith has never accomplished anything.

Passive faith is dead faith. Therefore, it is not a matter of trusting God to cast out the demons of curse. God has given US authority to cast out demons. It takes faith to cast out demons. We must believe that God's Word is true: that as believers we have authority over evil spirits, and when we command them: "Go, in the Name of Jesus," the demons must leave. Deliverance is faith in action.

9

STEPS TO BREAKING CURSES

As you have read through this book, you may have discovered evidence(s) of curses in your life. The following outline gives the necessary steps to become free from curses. We encourage you to act on each step by repeating the prayer-confessions aloud, and personalizing your prayers whenever appropriate.

Step One: **Affirm your relationship with the Lord Jesus Christ.** Overcome Satan with "the word of your testimony" Rev. 12:11, which is "the testimony of Jesus Christ" Rev. 12:17.

Prayer: Lord Jesus Christ, I believe with all my heart that You are the Son of God. You left Your throne of glory in heaven and became a man. You lived in this world and were tempted in all things like as we are, yet without sin. Then, You went to the cross and laid down Your life. Your precious blood was poured out for my redemption. You rose from the dead and ascended into heaven. You are coming again in all Your glory. Yes, Lord, I belong to You. I am Your child and heir to all your promises. You are my Savior, my Lord and my Deliverer. Amen.

Step Two: **Repent of all your sins (known and unknown)**; asking God's forgiveness through Jesus Christ.

Prayer: Heavenly Father, I come to You in an attitude of repentance. I ask you to forgive me of each sin that I have committed -- the ones I am aware of and those which I have not recognized. I am sorry for them all.

Step Three: **Renounce the sins of your forefathers.**

Prayer: Heavenly Father, I confess the sins of my forefathers. I now renounce, break and loose myself and my family from all hereditary curses, and from all demonic bondages placed upon us as the result of sins, transgressions and iniquities through my parents or any of my ancestors.

Step Four: **Accept God's forgiveness, and forgive yourself.**

Prayer: Heavenly Father, You have promised in Your Word that if I will confess my sins, You are faithful and just to forgive me of my sins and will cleanse me from all unrighteousness. (I John 1:9). I believe that You have forgiven me for Christ's sake; therefore, I accept Your forgiveness, and I forgive myself.

Step Five: **Forgive all others who have ever trespassed against you.**

Prayer: Lord, others have trespassed against me, but you have commanded me to forgive each person who has ever hurt me or wronged me in any way. I now make a quality decision to forgive (Name them, both living and dead). Also, I bless each of these whom I have forgiven and pray that they will have Your peace, joy and love in their lives.

Step Six: **Renounce all contact with cults, the occult and Eastern religions.**

Prayer: Father, I confess as sin and ask Your forgiveness for every involvement with cults, the occult and false religions. (Be as specific as possible.) I confess having sought from Satan's kingdom the knowledge, guidance, power and healing that should come only from You. I hereby renounce Satan and all of his works. I loose myself from him, and I take back all the ground that I ever yielded to him. I choose the blessing and refuse the curse. I choose life and not death.

Step Seven: **Destroy all books, objects and paraphernalia associated with any cult, occult or false religious source.**

Prayer: Heavenly Father, You are a jealous God, visiting the iniquities of the fathers upon the children unto the third and fourth generation of them that hate you. Therefore, I destroy all books and objects in my possession that are contrary to You and Your Kingdom. If there is anything in my possession that is not pleasing to you and gives any advantage to the devil, reveal this to me, and I will destroy it.

Step Eight: Cast out every demon of curse.

Warfare prayer: Satan, you have no right to my life and no power over me. I belong to God, and will serve Him and Him only. By the authority of my Lord Jesus Christ, I break the power of every evil curse that has come upon me. I command every demon of curse to leave me now: ancestral curse spirits, personal transgression curse spirits, witchcraft curse spirits and spoken word curse spirits.

[Note: Be as specific as possible in identifying spirits of curses.]

Step Nine: **Claim the blessing.**

Now that the curses are broken, and the demons of curse have been cast out, it is time to confess your blessings in the Lord. Know this: the grace of God enables you to stand unashamed in the presence of God Himself. Since you have God's favor, you are assured of His blessings.

Prayer: Heavenly Father, thank You for delivering me from every curse through the redemptive work of Your Son and my Savior, Jesus Christ. You exalt me and set me on high. You cause me to be fruitful and to prosper in everything. By Your hand of blessing I am a success and not a failure. I am the head and not the tail -- above and not beneath. You have established me in holiness. I am Yours, and I purpose to serve You and to glorify Your name.

[Note: Those in headship should bless those under their care. Let the pastor bless his people, the husband his wife, the parents their children. We have found it especially effective and deeply appreciated, after deliverance from curses, to speak a pastoral or fatherly blessing upon the one(s) delivered. It is a heart-moving experience for those who have never had a blessing spoken over them by persons in authority.]

God instructed Aaron and his sons to put His name upon the children of Israel and bless them. Let us use these same priestly words to speak blessings upon others.

> The Lord bless thee, and keep thee: The Lord make his face shine upon thee, and be gracious unto thee: The Lord lift up his countenance upon thee, and give thee peace.
>
> Numbers 6:24-26

AMEN!

THE SAINTS AT WAR

Too many Christian Soldiers are remaining inactive and ineffective in this hour of battle. This book is both a "call to arms" and an instruction manual to enable the Church, God's Army, to become aggressively militant toward its enemy, and that all the Saints of God might become SAINTS AT WAR.

Paperback 5.00

Booklets:

GOD WARNS AMERICA

In a night vision the author was shown three terrible judgments to come upon America: economic, bloodshed, and persecution of the Church. God reveals why and what must be done to avert the outpouring of His wrath.

Booklet 2.00

FAMILIAR SPIRITS

Brief, simple, but helpful scriptural information on this category of spirits and how to deal with them.

Booklet 2.00

SOUL TIES

Are a reality. Booklet explains what must be done to break them.

Booklet 2.00

CERDOS EN LA SALA

More than 500,000 copies of PIGS IN THE PARLOR, the recognized handbook of Deliverance, are continuing to help set people free around the world from demonic bondages. This Bestseller is now also available IN SPANISH — at the same price as the English edition.

Paperback 5.95

KINGDOM LIVING FOR THE FAMILY

A long awaited sequel to PIGS IN THE PARLOR, offering not mere unrealistic theories, but rather a Practical Plan for implementing divine order in the family, and preventing the need for deliverance.

Paperback 5.95

OVERCOMING REJECTION

Powerful help for confronting and dealing with rejection, which so often is found to be a root in individuals requiring deliverance. This book will help understand a tool commonly employed by the enemy in his attacks upon believers.

Paperback 5.95

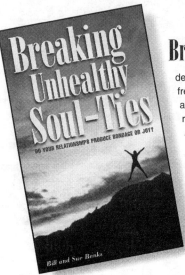

IMPACT BOOKS, INC.

Announces

The Exciting New Power for Deliverance Series:

Power for Deliverance; Songs of Deliverance
Power for Deliverance From Fat

Lives have already been changed by the powerful truths and revelations contained in these books as the author has taught them over the past seventeen years. These deliverance tools have been tested in the crucible of prayer room battles to free lives from Satan's control. You have tasted in this book the kind of dramatic accounts and truths which are to be found in the other volumes in this series.

Each book is just $5.95. When ordering add $1.50 postage and handling for the first book and $.50 for each additional title.

Available at your local Christian bookstore, library, or directly from:

Impact Christian Books, Inc.
332 Leffingwell Avenue, Suite 101
Kirkwood, MO 63122

THREE KINDS OF FAITH FOR HEALING

Many today have been taught that the only way to be healed is to personally have faith for their healing. It is implied, one must somehow 'work up' or develop enough personal *faith-to-be-healed*, and then healing will come. Many have also been told that the reason they remain afflicted is because of their lack of faith.

Such statements in addition to being utterly devoid of compassion, are terribly devastating to the poor hearers. One could never imagine Jesus saying something so heartless. Yet these things are often said today. Even those who have not heard these words spoken aloud have received them through implication from proud, spiritually 'superior' friends who believe that these sick individuals are somehow deficient in faith.

There is good news both for them and for us, because that teaching is wrong. There are more ways of being healed than just the one way, as we have been taught.

In this new book, Bill Banks presents a *revelation* of three main types of faith for healing illustrated in Scripture, and a fourth which is a combination of the other three.

Three Kinds of Faith For Healing   Paper   4.95

FOR ADDITIONAL COPIES WRITE:

Impac **Chris** *ian* **Books**

332 Leffingwell Ave., Suite 101
Kirkwood, MO 63122